Thread Magic

The Enchanted World of Ellen Anne Eddy

FIBER STUDIO PRESS

DEDICATION

To my parents, who gave me everything they had, and to the rest of the folk who have made family for me.

ACKNOWLEDGMENTS

Many people have helped me through this process; I need to thank them all: Mary Annis, for saving my grandmother's quilt from the trash and starting me down this road; Marilyn and Davey Packer, who gave me my first show at the Wild Goose Chase in Chicago; Robert Clarke and Susan Hecker, for their support and excellent critiques; Verena Rybicki, who is the Opener of Doors; Peter Vale of Vale Craft Gallery in Chicago, for his support and interest in quilts as art; the support group of FACET, for their critiques and for the stimulation of seeing all their wonderful works; John M. Walsh III, who is supporting art quilting by collecting the work of fine-art quilters; James P. Rowan, for allowing me to use his excellent photographs as models; Andrew's Company in Evanston, for their support; Karen Furnweger of the John G. Shedd Aquarium in Chicago, for permission to use their excellent publication; the people and organizations who have supported my work by purchasing it; my students, who let me know it was time to write this book by asking me for it; my proofreaders, Martin Johnson, Kathy Semone, Ellen Christensen, Elisa Dierks, Elaine Ferris, and Rebecca Brown; and the people at Fiber Studio Press, particularly Janet White and Laura M. Reinstatler, who have worked to make quilt books be art books.

MISSION STATEMENT

WE ARE DEDICATED TO PROVIDING QUALITY PRODUCTS AND SERVICE BY WORKING TOGETHER TO INSPIRE CREATIVITY AND TO ENRICH THE LIVES WE TOUCH.

FIBER STUDIO PRESS

CREDITS

Editor-in-Chief	Kerry I. Smith
Technical Editor	Laura M. Reinstatler
Managing Editor	Judy Petry
Proofreader	Leslie Phillips
Design Director	Cheryl Stevenson
Text and Cover Designer	Kay Green
Production Assistant	Claudia L'Heureux, Nancy Hodgson
Illustrator	Laurel Strand
Decorative Art	Ellen Anne Eddy
Photographer	Brent Kane

Page 80, the "Frogs!" edition of Aquaticus is shown courtesy of the John G. Shedd Aquarium in Chicago

Page 81, photo by James P. Rowan

Thread Magic:
The Enchanted World of Ellen Anne Eddy
©1997 by Ellen Anne Eddy

That Patchwork Place, Inc., PO Box 118
Bothell, WA 98041-0118 USA

Printed in Hong Kong
02 01 00 99 98 97   6 5 4 3 2 1

Library of Congress Cataloging-in-Publication Data

Eddy, Ellen Anne
    Thread magic : the enchanted world of Ellen Anne Eddy.
      p. cm.
    ISBN 1-56477-189-X
    1. Embroidery, Machine. 2. Machine quilting. I. Title.
TT772.E33   1997
746.44–dc21
                                            97-6040
                                              CIP

Table of Contents

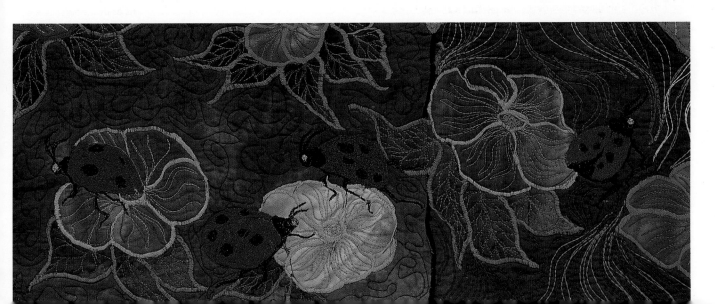

Finding the Beginning

Recalling beginnings is like stringing a strand of beads. Each bead sits separately in a dish, waiting to be selected, examined, and strung. The beads follow each other in a certain order in an effort to form a pattern that makes sense. Finding the exact beginning is tricky; one bead follows another. When people ask me when I started to machine embroider quilts, I find myself mildly perplexed by the question, looking at that bowl of beads, unsure where to begin.

Perhaps I started when I was five. My mother gave me a glitter wand that had a battery-lit star on top. I'm still playing with my glitter wand.

Or it could have been when I was thirteen and couldn't find clothing that fit. My mother got me a sewing machine, some fabric from the dime store, and a simple pattern. She ceremoniously dragged the trash can into the work room. "Not everything you do will work out, you know," she said. "We're not going to worry about that." Then she kindly left the room. I sat at the machine with the pieces of fabric in my lap. Soon, however, the pieces seemed to fall together by themselves under the needle.

Perhaps my work began with my grandmother's quilt top. My mother, who always cleaned by elimination, was not a quilter herself. My grandmother's unfinished red-and-white Kansas Trouble top was, for my mother, just trash—she tossed it. That day, when school got out, the kids of my neighborhood and I all streamed down the alley. The children next door spotted the quilt top in the litter. Their mother, our neighbor Mary Annis, rescued it. She had it quilted, and sent it to me when I was twenty-one. Of course I had to quilt after that.

Maybe I began when the same Mary Annis argued with my mother for three days that I needed art lessons. Finally my mother enrolled me in Mrs. Ryan's after-school art classes, worried that I would be disappointed but wanting me to have the experience of creation.

It could have been the time I fell in love with Amish quilts. They were wonderful, bold, and full of color. It wasn't until I pieced a top that I realized it had to be quilted and that I was a wretched hand quilter. Machine quilting wasn't even marginally acceptable at the time, but I started exploring ways to make it work for me.

Or did it all start the year I spent dealing with migraine pain? After awhile lying in a dark room, the mind drifts. During that year, I dreamed of a wolf who asked me to make a Moon-on-the-Mountain quilt. I made the quilt, and the pain lessened. Other quilts came in dreams and I responded by making them. The work began to lead me out of the pain and back to my life. The dream quilts still come and demand to be made. I've learned to listen.

We are always in the place of beginnings. Everything we've been leads us to the person we are becoming. Like a strand of beads, the memories exist separately, but combine to form the whole of who we are.

"I Paint What I See"

A Gahan Wilson cartoon shows an artist at his easel. Though the landscape before him is perfectly bare, his canvas is covered with all kinds of creatures. The little girl looking over his shoulder asks why he's painted them, and he answers, "I paint what I see."

The animal imagery I use seems to have a life of its own. My imagery is a vision, springing from the nonverbal, illogical, emotional center of my self. It knows the things I won't allow myself to know. It pictures the things I can't allow myself to say. I don't try to control it; I accept it instead as a gift.

There is a gut-level honesty within that vision that I've learned to honor. That honesty—about myself and my world—empowers my art, carrying me past the deficiencies of language and verbal logic. The images come, sometimes with phrases attached, sometimes not. The importance is not in understanding the images when they appear, but in interacting with them. If I could understand these issues verbally it would be enough to talk about them, but it isn't. Instead, the manipulation of an image in cloth and thread gives me enough power over the issues I'm engaging to enable me to choose my responses. I can suspend my panic, fear, and anxiety long enough to stand in the center of starkness, to look and respond through my art. I often don't understand the issue at hand until I'm done with the quilt.

Once I understand an image, I find my intent most often is to examine systems. I am fascinated by the checks and balances of societies. I work largely in animal imagery, because that is the imagery that springs out of my spiritual well. My colors reflect the natural world. I've come to know that the animals represent myself and people around me. This is how I see them. I paint what I see.

WHY I WORK BY MACHINE

First of all, I've always used a sewing machine. Sewing machines have been my constant friends since adolescence. The other deep and disturbing truth is that I am a poor hand sewer. When I fell in love with quilting, I tried to learn the worked-by-hand tradition and failed—my toe-catchers could have caught someone's elbow. When I started to play with traditional Amish quilts, I knew it had to be by machine. What I wanted to do was massively time consuming and too intense to consider working by hand. There were so many wonderful ideas and too little time.

But time is not the only factor. Machine quilting offers unique aesthetic qualities. From an artist's perspective, machine quilting presents an entirely different set of tools from piecing. Piecing is generally built on geometric shapes. The geometry offers bold designs of color and pattern in planes, but there are always limits. It's hard to make geometry feel organic; geometric leaves, flowers, bugs, and lizards never breathe.

The lines made by machine quilting closely resemble contour drawing. Contour line drawing is done by looking always at the subject, not at the paper. The artist creates an image by putting the pencil down at one point and never lifting it until the sketch is done. The result is full of movement, life, and excitement. It has the delicacy of a sketch and a sense of real motion. It lives.

The lines made by hand quilting are really dimples in the quilt surface. They define the pieced image, puffing it out, leaving it in relief. The line made by machine is a firm entity of its own. Once I knew I wanted to quilt living, breathing animals, there was no other choice. I had to work by machine.

In the traditional view of quilting, the quilting supports and accentuates the piecing. But, if we treat the pieced or appliquéd quilt top as a background for stitchery, all kinds of new effects are possible. The delicacy of thread work either accentuates the stitching lines or defines the design details that fascinate the viewer. It's an excellent change of focus.

I discovered wonderful potential in machine embroidery and in the incredible threads available. With embroidery, I can shade, round, and form a lifelike thread sketch until the image almost moves in my hands.

I was taught that nothing is impossible. If a job is too hard, too horrible, or too long, I have the wrong tools. I've had a vision of what I wanted and have searched for the tools to make it happen. The fusion of machine work—embroidery, appliqué, and quilting—has opened the road to possibilities.

Looking at the Quilts

Lurking behind all the frogs, lizards, and bugs, the element basic to my work is social commentary. My quilts divide into several series and themes, which I keep exploring. Though I have always refused to repeat any particular quilt, I've found I do rework important images. Certain animals now represent parts of myself or parts of my world. Sometimes, as I learn new techniques or as technology expands, I find myself revisiting a concept. An image gives me such joy that I find myself playing with and varying the idea, just to see what new places it will take me.

GUARDIANS

Guardians, most of them feathered or winged, have been powerful images for me. Most of these guardians are inner protectors; perhaps the most perilous dangers are the ones we face within ourselves. Who we are inside permits the chances we take with the world outside.

THE GREENING

33" x 46", ©1996.

Celebrating transformation is this quilt's theme. The woman is in the process of becoming a tree, just as the birds at her side are turning into leaves. Or is she changing from her tree form back into womanhood? When a transformation is in process, it's hard to tell. Change is a part of living. It deserves celebration, even if we're unsure where it's going.

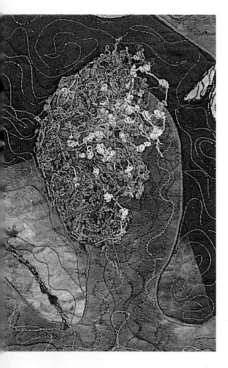

(Detail) For the hair, I piled three novelty yarns together on the quilt, covered them with Solvy, and then stitched over them with monofilament nylon thread. After stitching, I dissolved the Solvy in water.

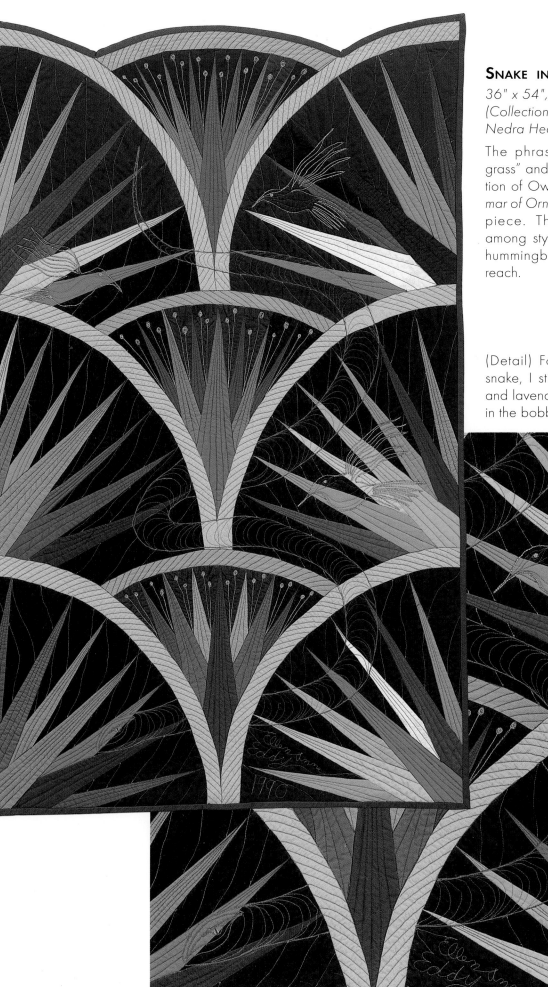

SNAKE IN THE GRASS

36" x 54", ©1990.
(Collection of
Nedra Hecker)

The phrase "snake in the grass" and the Egyptian section of Owen Jones's *Grammar of Ornament* inspired this piece. The snake winds among stylized reeds while hummingbirds flutter out of reach.

(Detail) For the birds and snake, I stitched with green and lavender ribbon threads in the bobbin.

LADY BLUE

39" x 51", ©1995. (Collection of Pat Carlson)

Lady Blue was commissioned by Pat Carlson, after we'd met in a mutual friend's kitchen in upstate New York. Commissions are a lovely challenge for an artist, blending someone else's vision with their own. Pat hunted for pictures of blue herons until she and I settled on the right lady heron to pose for this piece.

I did some cutaway appliqué, using green hand-dyed cotton for the rushes and iridescent organza for the water. I stippled the water with rainbow YLI and Candlelight thread to give it a reflective quality.

The heron's plumage is stitched in eighteen shades of rayon thread, ranging from white and pastels through grays to darkest blues. Couched chenille yarn offsets the dragonflies, which I embroidered from the back of the quilt.

(Detail) Stipple quilting in clear monofilament nylon thread defines this area without changing its coloration.

(Detail) I embroidered the frogs separately and then appliquéd them. I embroidered the reeds from the back of the quilt, using thick rayon and cotton threads in the bobbin.

(Detail) The butterflies were stitched onto tulle and Solvy stabilizer, trimmed, and then edged with rayon thread.

MORNING GLORIES

54" x 55", ©1995.

This quilt is about the abundance of the summers of one's life and the joy of being able to do what one wants and needs.

After embroidering the hummingbird, I stuffed it to add dimension. The butterflies' and the bird's wings are lace, machine made by embroidering on black glitter tulle stabilized with Sulky Solvy. Rayon thread details the leaves and flowers. I stipple quilted with flat metallics and iridescents. Novelty yarn, couched with monofilament nylon thread, winds through the piece, creating a visual path for the eye.

CROSSING THE RIVER

62" x 49", ©1996.

There are many myths about turtles and birds crossing water together. Sometimes the bird needs the turtle's help. Sometimes the bird just needs a temporary resting spot. Sometimes the turtle finds the whole thing too much.

This is a quilt made when the sky was fuchsia. I started with hand-dyed magenta cotton and appliquéd iridescent blue organza and tulle to the quilt sandwich for the water. I machine embroidered the bird and turtle separately, then appliquéd them to the quilt. For the reeds, I appliquéd green hand-dyed cotton, and stitched with rayon thread. Rayon, metallic, iridescent, and monofilament nylon threads create a lavish atmosphere.

(Detail) Yellow tulle and different shades of flat gold thread emphasize the light source around the Ibis' head.

(Detail) A rim of orange thread zigzagged on the tortoise's shell helps to define the light source within this quilt.

LIVING LAVA

29" x 52", ©1994.
(Collection of
Ellen Christensen)

Until I did the research for this quilt, I was unaware of the connection between volcanic action and the genesis of our world. Volcanoes, so violent, so frightening, and so out of control, are the primary force shaping our planet into continents and land masses. They are also unwitting artists in the act of creation.

Humans have emotional eruptions, explosions, and implosions. Perhaps within that personal inferno, we forge our selves. Fear turns into anger and anger into art. The transformation of anger into the energy to change empowers us to grow.

Hand-dyed cottons in grays, browns, and purples provide a cool background that offsets the lizards, aglow with oranges, reds, and coppers. The lamé flames add sizzle that, with the lizards, creates the impression of living lava. Smoky areas, created with nylon tulle and organza overlays, add to the effect of heat and fire. I machine embroidered this piece with nylon, rayon, metallic, and iridescent threads. For the stippling, I used variegated black-core metallic thread.

FIRED ELEMENTALS
39" x 63", ©1992.

Medieval people believed that salamanders were the living element of fire. They saw the salamanders leap out when logs were added to the hearth and were convinced that, since they were the color of flame, the salamanders themselves started the fire and kept it going. Here, they play in and out of the fireplace, in their element.

I pieced the fireplace from hand-dyed and commercial fabrics and used a walking foot for quilting. I layered twelve colors of organza onto the quilt in yellows, reds, and oranges; stitched the flames; and trimmed the organzas to different depths so the colors would shift and flicker. I machine embroidered the salamanders from the back with black-core metallic thread in reds, oranges, and burgundies.

I stitched flame shapes over layers of organza, and then cut away the excess. I finished the flame effect with a free-motion zigzag in yellow-orange threads.

IN THE CLEARING

Our society's conventions about beauty are painful sometimes, odd at all times. Our culture teaches children that there is no worse fate than to be different: to be too fat, too thin, too short, or too tall; in a way, to be themselves. Beauty is a matter of perspective. Insects that are strange and wondrously made could be the same bugs that haunt our dreams. Their intricacy, their delicacy, their beauty leads me to depict them over and over in my quilts, in an effort to confirm the beauty of true individuality.

(Detail) I stitched bands of many colors to create the faces of the cicadas.

(Detail) I wound metallic threads in the bobbin and embroidered the ladybugs from the back of the quilt.

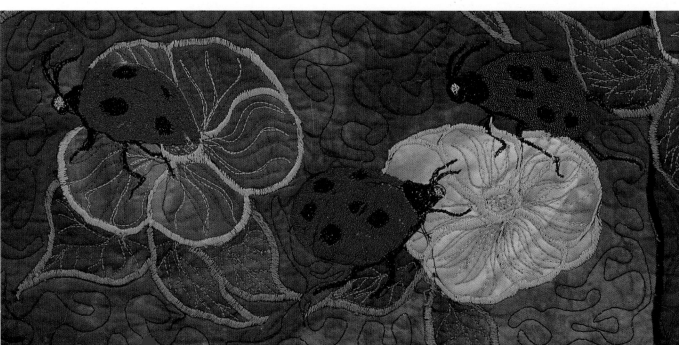

BY INVITATION ONLY

35" x 44", ©1993. (Private collection)

The social groups shown in this piece—the cicadas and the ladybugs—are fully busy with their parties, which seem to be by invitation only. In life, we rarely enjoy this type of exclusivity. We operate in each other's spheres with or without invitations.

I had a wonderful picture of cicadas that enticed me to make this quilt. I wanted to explore the possibilities of organza wings, and the cicadas provided the opportunity. Once I worked the tree and mushrooms into the piece, I realized that something needed to be on the ground as well. First came the flowers, then the ladybugs. When I was finished, I realized there were two very separate parties going on.

I used hand-dyed cottons and nylon organza for this piece. I machine quilted and embroidered with perle cotton and with rayon, monofilament nylon, iridescent, and metallic threads.

END OF SUMMER

18" x 21", ©1991. (Collection of Elizabeth Vale)

This demonstration piece portrays the last dandelions and dragonflies of summer in their final glory. I embroidered the entire quilt from the back. Beginning with a background of hand-dyed green-and-purple fabric, I embroidered the dragonfly directly onto the fabric with metallic threads.

Iridescent rainbow Candlelight thread defines the dandelion puffs, while perle cotton and novelty yarn make up the stems and leaves.

In the Clearing

38" x 33", ©1991. (Collection of John M. Walsh III)

Praying mantises fascinate me. I think it's because of their wonderful eyes and the way they move. The green hand-dyed cotton made a perfect clearing for this mantis and her community. I layered commercial green cotton over the hand-dyed fabric and drew a path of leaves and stems. I stitched the drawn shapes and then trimmed the excess commercial fabric to reveal the clearing. For the praying mantis and the other bugs, I embroidered from the back of the quilt. I selected several shades of gold thread for the sun rays and stippled with black YLI thread to create shadows. Couched novelty yarn completes the visual path.

(Detail) I constructed the spider web from thick iridescent rainbow Candlelight thread and thin YLI Single Ply thread.

TWILIGHT TIME

48" x 69", ©1993.

"Twilight Time" is about the joy of accepting the differences that make us unusual; odd and strangely made, yet wonderful. I started with two hand-dyed cottons rich with greens, purples, yellows, and magentas, machine piecing them in alternating strips. I cutaway appliquéd the leaves, and then machine embroidered the praying mantis directly onto the quilt. After adding borders, I embroidered and then appliquéd the remaining bugs.

For the stitching, I used novelty yarn plus metallic, rayon, perle cotton, and monofilament nylon threads.

(Detail) I used metallic thread to shade and highlight the praying mantis, creating the illusion of a light source within the quilt.

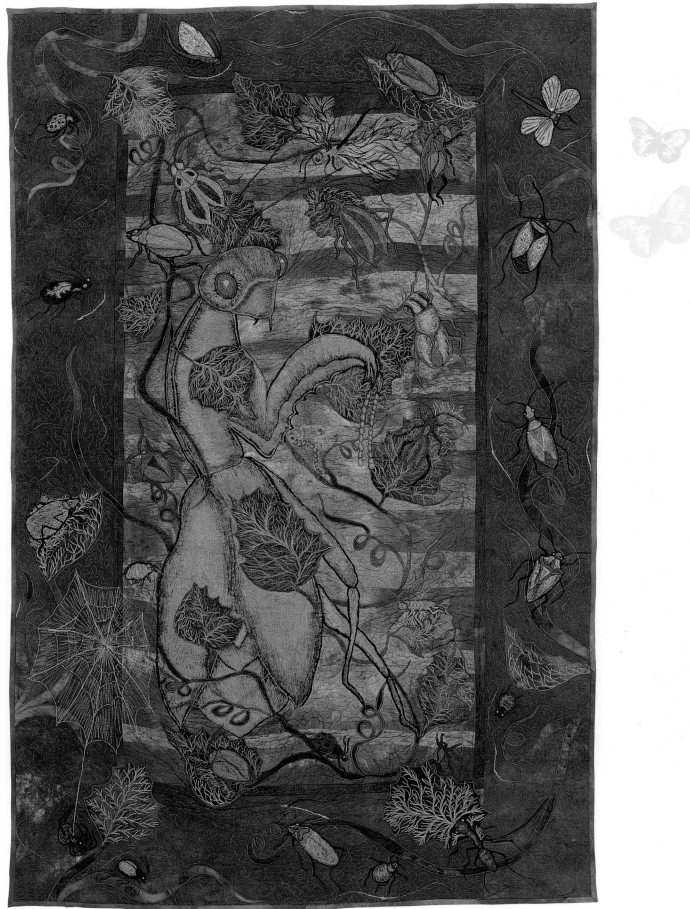

GROWING BETWEEN THE CRACKS

54" x 44", ©1994.

Most of what matters in life grows between the cracks. The bugs and the weeds thrive, but only in the unplanned spaces and for their own purposes.

For this piece, I used hand-dyed cotton in greens, yellows, and blues, with iridescent green organza for the leaves. Techniques include cutaway appliqué and machine-embroidered appliqués. I quilted and embroidered by machine, using metallic, rayon, iridescent, and monofilament nylon threads

(Detail) Purple perle rayon thread etches lines in the leaves, echoing the colors of the ant.

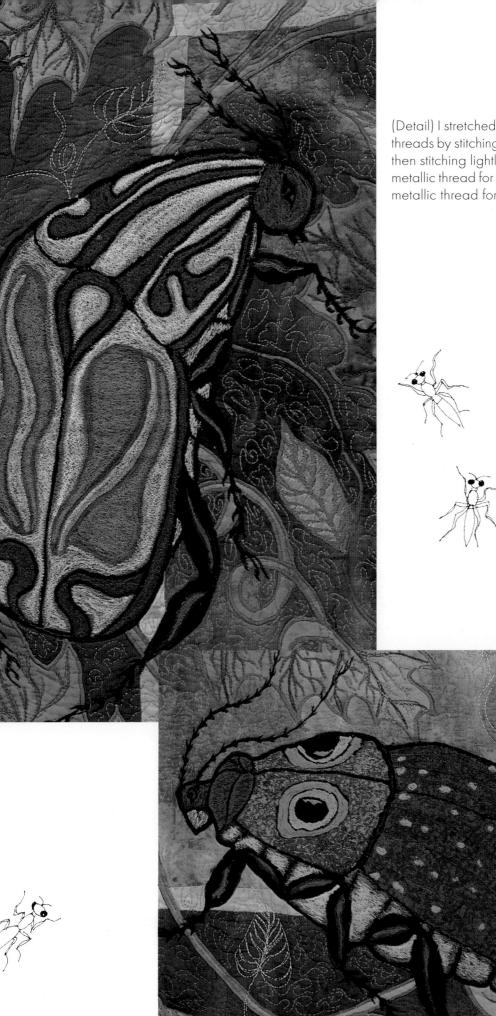

(Detail) I stretched a limited palette of metallic threads by stitching first with rayon threads and then stitching lightly over the rayon with black metallic thread for the bug on the left and gold metallic thread for the bug on the right.

A FEVERED SEASON

64" x 38", ©1994. (Private collection.)

The world in which bugs live mirrors our own. The insects' greed threatens their world; caterpillars have a chance to outgrow that behavior—if they live long enough.

The center panel of gold hand-dyed cotton suggested a parched landscape to me. When I first cutaway appliquéd the leaves, I had intended to fill them in with stitching. But as I worked, it became more important to leave some of them open as if they'd been attacked by the caterpillars. I appliquéd the flowers directly to the quilt top but embroidered the beetle separately and then appliquéd it.

I used one piece of hand dyed fabric for all the flowers, and embellished them with a variety of rayon threads.

(Detail) I originally drew this bug for "Growing Between the Cracks" (page 24), but it was too large. Instead, I gave it a quilt of its own.

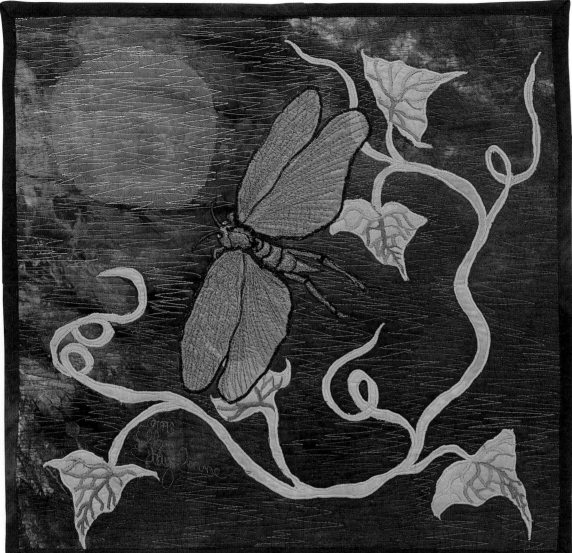

JUMP AT THE SUN

20" x 19", ©1995.

I made this quilt as a farewell for Khyam, my cat, who died in the summer of 1995. He left his life as he lived it, leaping joyfully from one experience into another.

A circle of golden tulle creates the light source in this quilt. I cutaway appliquéd the vines in bright green hand-dyed cotton. Using rayon, iridescent, and metallic threads, I embroidered the cricket separately, and then appliquéd it to the quilt.

(Detail) Iridescent organza and a range of metallic threads form the wings of this cricket.

SKIMMING THE SURFACE

36" x 47", ©1995.

Dragonflies live such surface lives: skimming, soaring, flitting, flying, and never having to deal with the consequences of where they land. I can't live that way, but it's tempting.

I appliquéd the clouds directly to the quilt, then garnet stitched them to add texture. The dragonfly bodies and wings are appliqués I embroidered separately and then stitched to the surface.

I embroidered the dragonfly-wing appliqués with metallic threads on a sandwich made of one layer of iridescent organza, two layers of sparkle tulle, and one layer of Solvy. I washed out the Solvy after completing the wings.

DAMSELLAS

18" x 26", ©1995.

The option to flit through life is very tempting. These summer insects have that luxury.

I began with a hand-dyed cotton that was a mix of blues, purples, and yellow greens. The entire horsetail plant was stitched from behind with perle rayon, perle cotton, and Madeira Decor threads. I stitched the damsel bodies directly onto the quilt using rayon, metallic, iridescent, and monofilament nylon threads. Novelty thread creates an impression of air currents.

(Detail) While I embroidered the back wings of the damsel flies directly onto the quilt, I made appliqués for the front wings to give a sense of depth. I embroidered them on tulle and Solvy, trimmed and edged, and then appliquéd.

Small Ponds

My work often features images of life in a pond. For me, ponds are endless sources of wonder, symbols of the ultimate community. In a community, everything interweaves to everyone's good or ill. No community member's actions are truly separate, because everyone is affected by the result of those actions. This delicate balance, allowing each individual within a community its own space and needs, is a mystery, one I'm always trying to explore from a different angle.

(Detail) The fly's wings and the leaves around the frog shimmer with iridescence. On the flower petals, I stitched small water drops of YLI Single Ply thread.

(Detail) Twelve shades of gold and blue thread and four kinds of black metallic thread give the frog's pupils a dynamic, reflective quality.

THE PROBLEM WITH PRINCES

53" x 62", ©1995.

We all have our toady qualities. These qualities are part of who we are, neither entirely good nor entirely bad. They are, however, socially limiting at times. The problem with the whole mating dance is that we expect someone of royalty who has no toadlike qualities of their own to completely transform us and ignore any swampy situations. I haven't noticed that this transformation normally happens, but I'm not worried by it. I'm contented to be the lovely lady toad that I am.

This quilt took six months to make. I used a commercial machine to embroider the frog, and it took me about one month. A friend loaned me her professional drip-fed iron, which convinced me of the importance of such an iron for constructing heavily embroidered quilts. Steaming the work after every two or three rows of stitching kept the frog and flowers flat. A miracle!

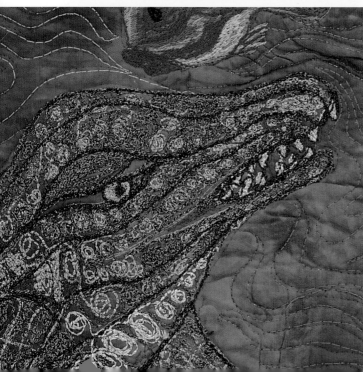

GONE FISHING

27" x 24", ©1993. (Collection of Mary A. Harper)

This quilt was inspired by Lewis Carroll's crocodile, who welcomes little fishes with gently smiling jaws.

I framed a blue cotton square with purple hand-dyed cotton, then appliquéd the coral strips directly onto the quilt. I stitched the crocodile and fish directly onto the quilt with a garnet stitch, using thick metallic threads for the crocodile and a small zigzag for the fish. I embroidered the anemones onto the coral strips. To complete the quilt and give it a wet look, I stipple quilted the entire surface with iridescent flat thread.

(Detail) Because it is smoother and wider, the flat metallic thread used in the eye and teeth of the crocodile reflects more light than the twisted Candlelight and Madeira Glamour threads used in the body.

LEAPFROG

28" x 22", ©1993. (Collection of Mary A. Harper)

I made these frogs as appliqués, then stitched them to the background of hand-dyed leaves and flowers. I shaded the foliage with perle cotton and rayon to make shadows.

I used a walking foot on my machine when I stitched the gold rays of the sun, the light source in the quilt.

(Detail) The green tulle appliquéd over the frog creates the illusion of shadows cast by leaves.

(Back of quilt) Because I used a straight garnet stitch on most of this quilt, I was able to stitch directly on the quilt sandwich, which created a visually exciting quilt back.

(Detail) A loose garnet stitch of perle cotton forms the alligator's scales.

LIVING ON THE EDGE

35" x 55", ©1993.

The frog and her family are in relative safety as the two crocodiles clash, clawing and snapping at each other. I started with two hand-dyed "light-source" pieces, cutting them into strips and piecing them alternately to give a sense of filtered light.

(Detail) To prevent distortion, I used a small zigzag when stitching the tadpoles and fish.

SKINNY DIPPING

48" x 56", ©1992. (Collection of John M. Walsh III)

When I was a child, my father's deepest love was fishing. Though I have never understood the sport itself, I came to love the woods and water, particularly looking through the water into the remarkably different world of fish and frogs. The aquatic world is a community of its own, organized by its own rules. Though it drifts unaware of us, it is ecologically fragile, and dependent on us for its survival. Like each of us, each water world is a tiny universe that can be vastly affected by conditions of the world at large.

For "Skinny Dipping," I began with two hand-dyed "light source" pieces, cut in strips. Alternating fabrics, I sewed the strips together to create the appearance of filtered light. Using thick threads in the bobbin, I stitched the frogs and fish directly onto the quilt from the back of the piece. I added a layer of blue organza to make the water glisten.

(Detail) When I laid blue organza over this frog he almost disappeared. I stitched current lines and cut away some fabric, and then he reappeared. Despite the organza that covers some of the frog, the viewer sees it as a whole.

(Detail) I chose straight-stitch garnet stitching for the frogs.

FALL FROLIC

11" x 11", ©1996. (Collection of Pamela M. Collins)

We find this toad frolicking through the leaves on a fine autumn day. I appliquéd the leaves to the quilt top before embroidering them. I worked in the opposite direction for the toad, embroidering first, then appliquéing to the quilt top.

CONTEMPLATIVE TOAD

29" x 25", ©1994.

Most people are as happy as they choose to be. I sometimes find contemplation dangerous; I might dig around my contentment until it's gone, instead of floating on the day's joys.

I chose a blue-and-aqua fabric for the background and olive green fabric for the water lily leaves. I stitched the dragonfly directly onto the quilt sandwich but made appliqués for the turtle, frog, and water bug. To create the water, I used three layers of sheer fabric in different blues. I appliquéd the pebbles with monofilament nylon thread in a free-motion zigzag to avoid covering the multicolored fabric.

From the beginning, I planned to include the frog in this quilt. I made the turtle at a demonstration, with no quilt in mind. When "Contemplative Toad" was in progress, I showed it and the turtle to students during a class I was teaching. One of the students picked up the turtle and said, "Aren't you going to add this?" She was right, so I did.

ENVY

59" x 58", ©1996.

Both the beauty and bad manners of swans are legendary. Beauty is an ephemeral enough state that I caution anyone who depends on it for self worth.

This is one of the first large quilts I made in which I embroidered images onto stabilizer instead of embroidering directly onto the three-layer "quilt sandwich." There are limits for both techniques, but I think it's easier to get a flat piece with the stabilizer method. It's certainly easier to move the work through the machine.

(Detail) Layers of organza under glitter tulle make ripples that circle the swan and fish.

HOPSCOTCH

38¹/₂" x 52¹/₂", ©1997

I keep returning to the image of frogs leaping for joy, because that joy is infectious. The frogs from rain forests are the most unbelievable colors. The first time I saw them in person I was totally knocked out. Of course I had to quilt them. Here they are in a playground of wet leaves.

FISH IN THE STREAM

The "Fish in the Stream" series was clearly influenced by my father's love of game fishing. He fished as a meditative exercise rather than as a sport. I never picked up his need to catch fish, but I caught his joy in their watery worlds and wild movements. For me, fish in water have become a metaphor for how people move through their lives.

(Detail) Before I began "Wake-Up Call," I made this oriole in a demonstration. When the idea for the quilt came to me, I knew she should be singing from the top branch.

(Detail) This fish generates visual movement by "swimming into" the quilt.

(Detail) Glitter tulle applied over the body of this fish indicates water currents.

WAKE-UP CALL

58" x 71", ©1995.

Spring and personal rebirth are not immediate transformations. Both occur in layers. Winter's cold, and spiritual darkness, are banished in increments. Relief has its heralds, however; we get our wake-up calls and respond as best we can, depending on how deeply we're stuck in the mud.

I embroidered all the fish on one piece of fabric, cut them apart, and then appliquéd them to the background of alternating strips. The visual texture of hand-dyed cotton works perfectly for the branches, while layers of organza and tulle emphasize water currents. I appliquéd the floating leaves and "dusted" them with metallic thread.

BREAKING THE ICE

35" x 66", ©1993.

This is an early spring quilt. I started it in February and completed it over a spring that was awfully cold, both inside and out. It is a reminder that there is an end to all winters, even emotional ones. Given time, the ice does break and life goes on.

This is one of the last quilts on which I zigzag embroidered onto the quilt sandwich itself. Embroidering the fish distorted the background immensely, and surgery was a necessity. I made cuts across the areas that puffed up, then overlapped and stitched the edges to close the cuts and flatten the quilt. Of course, once something has been stitched as closely as this, I can cut it apart and sew it back together with very little harm done. It's made more of thread than of fabric. I camouflaged the cuts with appliquéd leaves.

I used every green metallic thread I could find, as well as some pinks, silvers, and corals for the fish's belly. Even greens that ordinarily clash blend when embroidered.

FATHER OF ALL FISHES

25" x 40", ©1990. (Collection of Robert Clarke)

This is a portrait of my friend Michael Renziuk, who died in 1983 at the age of thirty-one. I had tried to make several memorial pieces for Michael. They all involved photo transfer, and they were all dreadful. In the midst of that muddle, this quilt happened so easily I barely remember working on it. It sold before I could have it photographed, and when I borrowed the quilt for a photo session and put it on the wall, I realized that, in essence, the fish *was* Michael. It was a real lesson for me—understanding that I do not have to comprehend what I'm working on at the time to do the right thing.

Michael loved the spotlight. Here, he basks in it.

I stitched the fish from the back of the quilt with gold perle cotton. On the front of the quilt, the area of light value in the background fabric makes the fish appear to glow from within.

Spring Running

46" x 80", ©1994.

Salmon "run," driven by instinct. This instinct can be personally dangerous for them, even leading to their destruction. For a salmon, it might be better if they had the option to swim idly next to the shore.

So much of life is organized by biological rhythms and patterns, yet it seems to be a harsh struggle: hard to be, to do, to produce. Salmon are caught by the instinct. The frog, not burdened by the salmon's self-destructive programming, has the option of observation, of standing by the shore and watching.

I would rather be a human *being* than a human *doing*. Yet the urge to produce grabs me by the throat from time to time. I respond to it almost by instinct; I run with it, struggle against it, break down under it, float over it. The real struggle is remembering that there is a day-to-day choice.

Since I was unable to find good salmon pictures when I started this quilt, I used a rubber salmon I found at a nature store. It was perfect! I could turn it to any angle and really see what the fish looked like from the back or side or front. Since then, I regularly haunt toy stores for good models.

I drew and stitched the three salmon as one unit because their bodies overlapped.

A wide zigzag stitch, done free-motion style, adds delicacy to the ferns.

SCHOOLING

59" x 47", ©1996.

I embroidered all three of these fish as one unit, but as I laid them out on the quilt top, I realized that one needed to be cut away. Because the fish were heavily embroidered with a free-motion zigzag stitch, the newly cut edges would be prefinished and therefore secure. So I cut the fish apart and placed one opposite the others.

In nature, water bugs are just brown and black, but here some green and purple threads mixed in provide more interest. I try never to be so firmly placed in reality that I miss a beautiful color combination.

(Detail) The background fabric was vastly distorted by the time I was done embroidering these fish. But once I trimmed the fabric from the edges, the fish were perfectly flat and ready to appliqué.

TWILIGHT POND

69" x 57", ©1996. (Collection of Robert Clarke and Susan Hecker)

This quilt is about meeting an old friend, who I found was a friend no longer. The meetings of old friends can be very disappointing. Were the life changes between us too overwhelming? Or had time rewritten my memories so that I saw that person in a softer light? Either way, real contact shattered whatever illusions were left. As much as I value truth, sometimes illusions are much more comfortable.

I stitched the fish in reds, golds, and purples, starting with the darker colors over their backs and ending with the pale shades at their bellies. I chose to make the leaves large, because I wanted to start simplifying the backgrounds of my quilts. I emphasized the leaves with layers of zigzag stitching in rayon thread.

(Detail) I originally planned to stipple the areas where I had cut away the organza, but the contrast of no stitching made a stronger statement.

(Detail) These dragonflies, left over from "Skimming the Surface" (page 28), are perfect placed among the leaves. I am delighted when I have extra embroidered appliqués. They always find the right home.

UNDER THE SEA

I am always astonished and amazed by the opulence of the undersea world: beautiful, rich beyond belief, dangerous, treacherous, much like the possibilities for our own lives. We're offered a banquet table of options, both good and ill. In the end we reach for what we want, whatever fulfills our personal myths and our beliefs about ourselves.

CORAL SEA
47" x 30", ©1994.

This quilt is about distance within relationships. I find relationships a constant puzzle. Sometimes I feel like I'm missing a piece, and sometimes I think I can see more clearly for not being part of a situation. Even within the beauty of realized dreams, we still live with disappointment. Those disappointments color everything we do and everything we are. The fish are part of each other's world. Are they happy? Who can tell? Appearances have little to do with how life feels to the people involved. Alone or partnered, we design our own joys and sorrows. Most of life is neutral. What matters is our response.

The light source in this quilt reminds me of the glowing treasure chests that open and close in aquariums. Here, bubbles of iridescent organza float to the surface. I originally appliquéd them with white thread, but that made too hard a line, so I shaded the bubbles' edges with fabric markers in greens, purples, and yellows.

(Detail) Analogous pinks, reds, purples, oranges, and yellows add richness to this underwater scene.

Secret Garden

54" x 50", ©1994.

This is a portrait of an old friendship. Sometimes friendship works only if it has its own built-in barriers and guardrails. Sometimes the only way to be close is to be well armored within the secret places where we risk intimacy. Without the barriers, friendship is too dangerous to contemplate.

This quilt was my first exploration of machine-embroidered appliqué. I selected lobsters because I knew the shape would be a good test to see if I could control distortion. Anything in a C shape tends to buckle in on itself.

Once I cut away the excess fabric, I knew it was a success. The lobsters puffed slightly, as though they had been stuffed, but there were no wrinkles or major puckers. Chenille novelty yarn and the yellow-green appliquéd reef direct the visual path around the clown fish and anemones.

(Detail) The lobsters, created with twenty-two shades of thread, started with purples and continued through reds, oranges, and pinks, with a final "dusting" of metallic copper thread.

BEYOND THE BREAKERS

52" x 71", ©1994.

The reefs are a safe place for the turtles to grow. But over time, these habitats become unsafe simply by being too small for the maturing turtles' needs. What was once a haven becomes a trap. We grow, we change, or we die. Going beyond safe, well-known barriers is the price of autonomy, growth, and life itself.

    This piece is larger than my usual quilts; I found I needed to step back to see the piece. In doing so, I realized the larger figures seemed incomplete, so I added smaller ones to help direct the flow of the composition. Finally, I took the quilt outside, hung it on the clothesline where I could really see it, and discovered what I needed to do. Most design problems come from not being able to see how the elements of a quilt relate to each other. Once we can see how the elements of a quilt interact, our innate sense of design tells us what to do next.

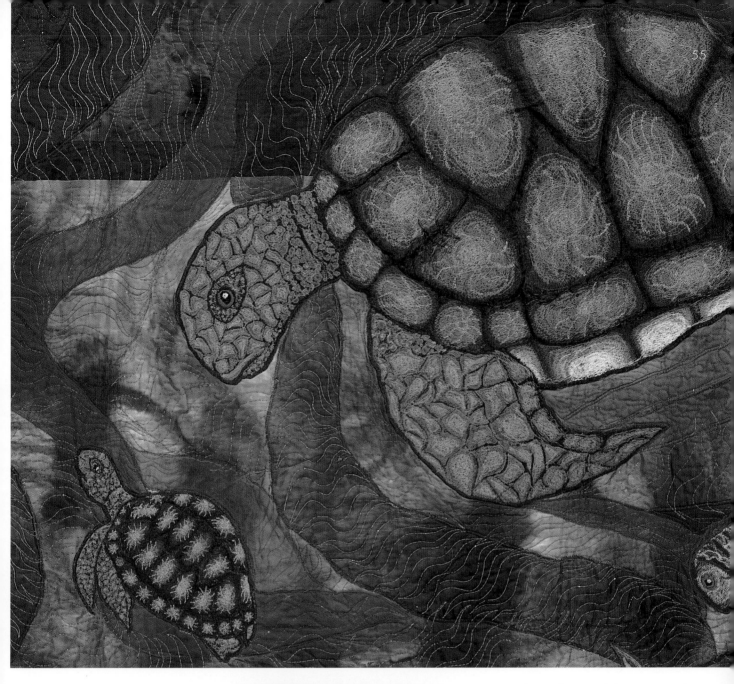

(Detail) I used the same colors for both the mother and baby turtles, but I expanded the hue and thread ranges for the larger turtle to keep the palette active and inviting.

(Detail) This parrotfish shows the difference between shaded stitching (in the fish's face) and distinct rows of color (in the scales).

Coral Reef

49" x 36", ©1992. (Collection of Judah Greenzad)

This turtle quilt is about nurturing and mothering instincts. I've finally had to face the fact that I probably won't be having a child of my own this time around. Looking past the feelings of grief and failure connected with that, lately I've come to see that the maternal aspect of womanhood is not simply relegated to mothers. There's the need to nurture myself, the women I work with and teach, the children who stumble into my life, and my small corner of the world. Like the mother turtle, the trick seems to be to give what is needed and let the children go toward the light in their own way.

I pieced the reefs from hand-dyed and marbleized cotton. I machine pieced the background, alternating strips of two hand-dyed pieces. I used flat metallic thread for the appliquéd and embroidered anemones among the reeds.

(Detail) Different varieties of garnet stitch in thick rayon and cotton threads make up the body of this turtle.

SILENT SPLENDOR

29" x 42", ©1990. (Collection of Peter Vale)

In this early study, I straight stitched the fish using rayon threads on hand-dyed fabric. The gold and orange threads of the fish vibrate against the complementary blue background.

I chose a commercial black fabric for the back of "Silent Splendor." Wispy on the front, the rayon thread is electric on the back, creating a "night side."

Underwater Collection

"Angel," "The Reef 2," and "Crabby Days" belong to a series of small underwater landscapes and underwater denizens. All three of these pieces were experiments in using and fusing sheers. I was reluctant to fuse sheers until I realized that excess glue could be ironed onto another piece of fabric. After stippling, the glue that remains is no longer visible. (See "Fused Apliqués" on page 97.)

 **ANGEL**
13" x 13", ©1996.

THE REEF 2
13" x 13", ©1995.

CRABBY DAYS
15" x 15", ©1995.
(Collection of Necia Wallace)

Equipping the Studio

Please keep in mind that the technical advice in this section is based on personal experience and what I've learned from my students. Each sewing machine is a little different. People are too. The results that please me are just that: results that please me. There are no rights or wrongs. My methods are simply techniques right for me and for my work.

You may find some techniques work better for you than others. Honor your experiences. Keep track of them. When you see experts disagreeing about methods or you find yourself disagreeing, look for the differences in their work that account for those disagreements, and then choose what will work best for you. Try what I suggest, but don't be afraid to experiment. In the end, you'll blaze a trail to the kind of work you want to do. I'll just put up some signposts.

Usually I'm not much impressed by brand names. If I list a product by brand, it means that for my needs, I've found it superior to or different from anything else available, and it offers a remarkable difference in ease and usability. I mention specific thread names in examples so that you can develop a sense of what each looks like when you examine the photographed quilts.

MATERIALS

Because heavily embroidered quilts are meant for the wall and must hang flat, it's important that fabrics be used on the straight grain so they won't stretch. Knits and crepes are poor choices for quilts, as both tend to stretch. The fabrics that work best for me are hand-dyed pima and Kona cotton, organza, and tulle.

Cottons

Pima cotton is tightly woven from fine cotton yarn. Evenly grained, it is dense, strong, smooth, and a little shiny. Kona cotton and print cloth are rougher and made from thicker yarn, and they take dye more boldly than pima cotton.

Once I discovered hand dyeing, the necessity of creating a pieced land-scape from prints and solids evaporated. Now, while I often frame a piece with borders to give it more structure, sunlight, water, woods, and trees are conveniently included in the varied colors of the hand-dyed fabric.

When I have a quilt in mind, I often dye several pieces of fabric to get the one that's perfect. Other times, a piece of fabric suggests exactly the quilt it should become. Since each hand-dyed fabric is unique, a quilt made with it has a singular stamp from the beginning. The problem with hand-dyed fabric is that nothing else is quite so wonderful, and nothing matches it as well as more hand-dyed fabric. I use it almost exclusively for tops, backings, and bindings.

Hand dyeing provides me with limitless fabric choices. Any effect I want, I can dye.

Sheers

Sheer fabrics, such as chiffon, organdy, and net, work wonderfully as overlays because of their lightweight body. They come in all colors and fibers, and in several densities. I use nylon sheers most often, but silk is easier to dye and to press. Some sheers have iridescent threads and patterns running through them. When you cover a fabric with a sheer, the tone and shade of the underlying fabric changes, but subtly.

Net is a woven fabric that has been twisted, or if the net is made from nylon, molded, to make holes. Tulle is the sheer, small-holed version; when laid over another fabric, it is almost invisible, except for the subtle change in tone and shade it causes. The most natural-looking effects come from placing layers and layers of tulle over another fabric. In nylon, tulle comes in a range of colors, and in silk it is available in white and ecru. Nets and tulles are also available with different kinds of glitter glued on or woven in.

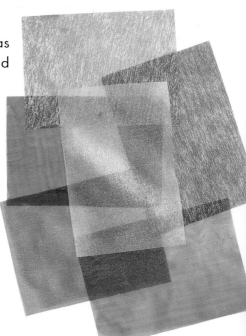

Use sheers to shade and tone each other or the background of a quilt.

Because of its high transparency, tulle shades more subtly than other sheers.

Stabilizers

I used to do all my stitching directly onto the quilt sandwich. This technique led to wonderfully exciting quilt backs, but it also distorted quilts ferociously. Lately I've been working the embroidery on just the quilt top with a layer of stabilizer underneath. Once I've finished the embroidery, I layer the quilt top with batting and a backing fabric and then quilt lightly around the images with monofilament nylon thread. The backs aren't as wonderful, but the distortion is much less severe. Even if I embroider directly onto the quilt sandwich, I put a layer of stabilizer between the top and batting to keep the layers from buckling.

My favorite stabilizers are nonwovens. Stitch-n-Tear makes a great base for small pieces. With large pieces, it tends to tear along the stitching, so I use an iron-on nonwoven interfacing that is slightly less stiff than Stitch-n-Tear. For my machine-embroidered appliqués, I draw patterns directly onto Totally Stable, a lightweight nonwoven interfacing with a backing similar to freezer paper. I iron it onto the fabric and remove it when the embroidery is complete.

Battings

The batting I use needs enough body and stability to support intense stitching. I like cotton and mostly cotton battings best because they cling to the fabric and don't beard or poke through the stitches the way some polyester battings do. The cotton batting of Grandma's time needed to be quilted every ¼" to ½". Most contemporary cotton battings allow the quilter more leeway. Mountain Mist Blue Ribbon Cotton should be quilted every 2" to 3", Fairfield Cotton Classic every 4" to 6" inches, and Warm and Natural and Morning Glory Old Fashioned Cotton Batt every 6".

I most often choose Old Fashioned Cotton Batt because it's stable, flat, and responds like a thin flannel blanket. It's made of cotton that has been needle-punched into a nylon core.

I've used all the battings I've mentioned to good effect. There are always new battings being made available. If you want to try the latest products, look for low-loft battings that don't stretch but that do cling to fabric.

THREADS

Embroidery Thread

Embroidery threads are a necessity for the kind of stitching I do. Regular threads are three-ply (three yarns twisted together), and are made for sewing seams. They bulk up quickly if you stitch over an area more than once. Embroidery threads are two-ply. They lie flat and don't jam under the machine as consistently as regular thread does. Almost any embroidery thread can be used easily with little fuss.

Embroidery threads are divided into several categories. Thread weight and fiber content identify each thread's best use. The higher the thread-weight number, the thinner the thread. For example, #5 pearl cotton is very thick. Some threads come as thin as #70.

Any #30- or #40-weight thread is thin enough to go through a machine needle. For solid embroidery, #40-weight is the better thread. The #30-weight thread is thicker than #40; it fills in quicker, but it doesn't blend as well. I would most likely use #30-weight thread for outlining or stippling.

Rayon, polyester, and cotton embroidery threads come in a vast range of colors. Rayon and polyester threads are shinier than cotton, but otherwise they're interchangeable. Polyester is the least breakable, but the colors don't blend as well as rayon or cotton.

An assortment of cotton, rayon, and polyester #40-weight embroidery threads

Metallic Thread

Thin metallic threads come in three varieties: wrapped, flat, and flecked. Most often, metallic threads are made from Lurex, which is an aluminum-based fiber coated in plastic. Lurex is strong, rich in color, and never corrodes.

Wrapped threads have a nylon or a polyester core, which is wrapped in Lurex. Flat threads are thin strands of Lurex. "Flecked threads" are what I call threads made of twisted Lurex and polyester yarns. These flecked threads have white or black cores.

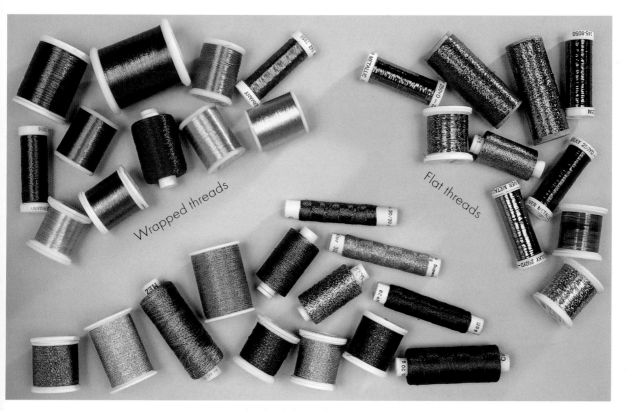

Wrapped threads

Flat threads

Flecked threads

Thick Thread

Use thick threads in the bobbin.

Thick threads come in a variety of colors and are made from a variety of materials. In rayon, you can find both smooth and twisted thick threads. If you want a natural fiber, #8 perle cotton is similar to thick rayon but is less shiny. Several brands of thick, twisted metallic threads are available, including YLI Candlelight, Kreinik 1/8"-wide metallic ribbon, and Madeira Glamour.

Novelty Yarn

Don't neglect the incredibly beautiful novelty yarns available, such as bouclé and chenille. Novelty yarns are wonderful for drawing a visual path through the design. Couch them to the quilt with monofilament nylon thread.

You can find novelty yarns in yarn shops, through thread suppliers, and in sewing-machine stores. Many fabric stores and quilt shops carry a limited supply.

Utility Thread

MONOFILAMENT NYLON is a thread I use constantly to quilt and stipple and to couch novelty yarns. YLI, Sulky, and Madeira all make versions of this thread, usually about #.003 or #.004 weight.

CORDONNET, OR BUTTONHOLE TWIST, in polyester, silk, and cotton, works well for outline quilting and is available in a larger range of colors than you might find in perle cottons or rayons.

GIMP is a very heavy cotton thread I use to edge three-dimensional appliqué and machine-made lace. It comes in black and white.

THREADFUSE is a polyester thread that contains a strand of fusible nylon. I put it in the bobbin when I sew the binding to the back of a quilt. When I turn the binding to the quilt front, I have a stitched line of fusible glue that allows me to fuse the binding in place. The binding stays flat while I topstitch the edges.

I'll discuss how different brands and varieties of thread can be used after we've looked at the mechanics of machine stitching.

Monofilament nylon, ThreadFuse, and gimp are neutral-colored threads, usually not highly visible on a quilt.

TOOLS

Here is some basic technical information about sewing machines, including mechanical adjustments and details that make thread magic work. A big part of what I do depends on my machines. They are my partners.

Sewing Machines

The Dream Machine

The ideal machine would have the following features:

- ❧ Option to disengage or lower the feed dogs. Moving feed dogs push and pull your work out of your hands. It's nice to be able to drop them out of the way.

- ❧ Excellent stitch quality. Your stitch is your drawing line. If it doesn't look straight and smooth, it distracts the eye.

- ❧ A zigzag stitch. This stitch is necessary for many kinds of embroidery.

- ❧ Removable, adjustable bobbin case. There are excellent machines with drop-in, adjustable bobbin mechanisms, but I find the tension on an old-fashioned metal bobbin case more reliable.

- ❧ Bobbin winder on the outside. I've not seen a machine that winds bobbins through the needle do well with delicate or specialty threads. The thread either breaks or jams.

- ❧ A darning foot with an opening large enough that you can see the stitching.

- ❧ A walking foot. A regular presser foot can drag on the upper fabric layer while the feed dogs push the bottom layer. This causes distortion and alignment problems with appliqué and quilting. A walking foot allows the fabric layers to move at the same rate.

- ❧ An optional needle-down function. It's helpful to have the needle stop automatically in the down position if you pause while stitching.

- ❧ Several side-to-side needle positions. Most machines have a center position, and two additional positions for stitching both right and left of center. A few machines allow you to move the needle in infinite positions from left to right.

- ❧ An edging and/or blind-hem foot is helpful for sewing a line of stitching right next to a fabric edge.

- ❧ Additional utility stitches, such as blind hem, fagoting, and double-knit stitches, are very helpful.

The Real Machine

Since different machines are good at different functions, it's important to know which ones have the functions you want. I have several machines set up constantly in my studio space. My Bernina 930 is a mechanical machine (not computerized). Its oscillating hook and its stitch quality make it ideal for basic free-motion stitching and thread-magic techniques. My Pfaff 1475 has a fabulous walking-foot mechanism that I love for piecing and construction. The 1475 is computerized, and I use it to make quilt labels. My Singer 20 U is a commercial machine that's so fast it threatens to eat babies and cats, but it can zigzag day in and day out at speeds that would freeze the Bernina. I also have a Baby Lock Quilt and Craft machine to take to the classroom. Between the four of them, I have what I need.

For those who have to choose one machine or who can't buy a new one right now, there are answers to an imperfect reality. For feed dogs that don't drop, cover them, either with a plate made for the purpose or with masking tape, and set the stitch length at 0. The stitch length controls the speed of the feed dogs. The longer the stitch, the faster the feed dogs must move to advance the fabric. With the stitch length set at 0, the feed dogs don't move much, which makes free-motion quilting easier.

As mentioned earlier, specialty threads don't work well with machines that wind the bobbin through the needle. If necessary, you can wind bobbins by hand.

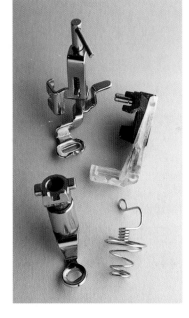

There's a darning foot for almost every kind of machine.

If your machine's darning foot doesn't allow you to see the stitching, or if your machine doesn't have a darning foot, don't despair. All kinds of alternatives are available. If a darning foot isn't made for your machine, often you can use one with an adapter. For very old machines, like Featherweights, sometimes the best answer is a darning spring, which is a small wire attachment that sits on the needle bar and coils around the needle. Find a mechanic or dealer who knows machines and accessories. There are all kinds of options, gadgets, and marvels available.

Sewing Machine Hygiene

Sewing machines are like cars—they need regular maintenance. When they work well it's like a dream, but when they don't, it's a real nightmare.

Clean and oil your machine after every ten hours of use; doing so more often doesn't hurt. What I put a machine through is demanding, so I often clean and oil a machine after emptying three bobbins.

Change to the right kind of needle for each project, before you start. A dull or bent needle or the wrong needle for the thread and fabric isn't healthy for your machine and won't give you the results you want.

Get a tune-up for your machine at least once every two years, whether you use it or not. Extra care is simply wise. Your sewing machine is your partner, your best friend, and your tool. It needs your help to do the job well.

Bottom-Tension Adjustment

You'll sometimes want to use a thick thread in your bobbin, and you'll need to adjust the thread tension to do so. The thread tension is not regulated only by that top dial on your sewing machine. Sewing machines make what is called a *lock stitch* by twisting the top and bottom threads together. When the mechanic adjusts the tension, she's most likely adjusting the bobbin (bottom) tension as opposed to the top tension.

Your mechanic adjusts the bobbin case every time she cleans, oils, and times your machine. It's an excellent idea to leave that adjustment just as she set it. I recommend having a second bobbin case or housing to use for thick threads. (Most bobbin cases aren't expensive.) The little screw that holds the tension is fragile and will only move so many times before stripping its threads. It's easier to make an adjustment once for each bobbin case, changing cases as needed. Mark the outside of one case with a drop of nail polish for easy identification.

Bobbin-Case Models: Most sewing machines manufactured prior to 1960, including Berninas, Pfaffs, and some Vikings and Whites, have a removable metallic housing, where the bobbin sits. That's the bobbin case.

The most common bobbin-case mechanism is a generic class 15. It fits many machines, although some machines require a special type of bobbin case. Ask your sewing machine dealer or mechanic for recommendations.

Adjust the tension by turning the screw on the side of the case: lefty loosey, righty tighty. To check for the correct tension, suspend the bobbin and bobbin case by grasping the thread. Jerk the thread slightly. If the bobbin turns one revolution in the case, the tension is correct.

Drop-In Bobbin Models: Newer Singers, Elnas, New Homes, and some Vikings and Whites have bobbins that drop into the machine. There is a housing inside the machine where the bobbin sits that can be adjusted, or in some cases, bypassed. There is a screw on the side that can be adjusted: lefty loosey, righty tighty. Check the manual, talk to your mechanic, and experiment.

Bobbin cases

Drop-in bobbin housing

The Three-Point Cure for "Tension Headache"

Most tension headaches aren't caused by incorrect tension settings. Instead, the thread is probably not under tension at all. If this is the case, the problem can usually be fixed in one of these three ways:

RETHREAD THE MACHINE, TOP AND BOTTOM. As you sew, the thread sometimes jumps out of tension. Or you could be having problems because the machine wasn't threaded properly to begin with. Make certain the presser foot is up when you thread the machine.

CLEAN AND OIL THE MACHINE. Some machines are so accurately balanced that a tiny bit of fluff can pull them out of line. Clean the machine with a pastry brush, a computer vacuum, or canned air, then oil it, referring to your machine's manual.

CHANGE THE NEEDLE. If the needle is bent or nicked, the machine will produce dreadful stitches or skip stitches altogether. Sometimes it's not obvious that a needle is damaged. Try replacing it, just in case. Ninety-nine times out of a hundred, this will save a trip to the mechanic.

Needles

Needles can cause endless problems if they're damaged or inappropriate for a particular use. The wrong needle can cause skipped stitches and broken threads, not to mention torn hair. Needle types are a mystery to many, but a little sewing history may unravel it for you.

In the beginning, there were only woven fabrics and "Sharp" needles. Sharp needles pierced the fibers, which was just fine with woven cloth.

Then the polyester double-knit plague swept the land. Survivors remember wearing heavy, sweaty pantsuits that had snags along the seam line. In an effort to relieve those snags, the "Ball-Point" needle was developed. The rounded point went between the yarns instead of piercing and snagging them.

The double-knit plague subsided, but the genie was out of the bottle. There were many kinds of knits after that. They didn't snag the way polyester did, but a Sharp needle still didn't work well for them. So engineers developed the "Universal" needle, shaped like a Sharp, with a mildly rounded point. It works reasonably well for all kinds of fabrics, including both wovens and knits. Like all compromises, it has its limits; Sharps still work best for wovens, and Ball Points work best for knits. The Universal is the most common needle available today.

Most Sharps are not labeled with that name. All kinds of Sharps are available; it helps to know the differences among the most common types.

➷ "Topstitching" needles have eyes that are large enough to handle cordonnet, or buttonhole twist. They're perfect for fragile threads, such as silks and metallics.

➷ "Denim" needles have regular eyes and a slick coating for punching power.

➷ "Quilting" needles are—guess what—our original Sharp needles revisited. For machine embroidery on woven fabric, quilting needles make the cleanest, best stitch—they have "piercing power." For general quilting purposes, good quilting needles are essential.

Here are my sewing machine needle recommendations:

Most European machines: Use sharp-pointed Schmetz needles, sizes 80–90, labeled "topstitching," "denim," or "quilting." I prefer the topstitching needles.

New Home machines: Use Schmetz "embroidery" or Metalfil needles, sizes 80–90. These needles have a slight ball point, but this machine likes them, and the manufacturer recommends them. Whatever works!

If you can't find the recommended needles, the machine won't blow up. Universal needles, sizes 80–90, work in a pinch. The stitch won't be as good, but it won't be fatal.

Singer machines: Use Red Band needles, sizes 14–16. A Singer machine can take a Schmetz needle, but a European machine should never be fitted with a Singer needle. Singer needles are slightly longer than Schmetz needles and can badly scar the hook of the machine.

Note: Some quilters use spring needles—which are just what the name implies, needles with an attached spring—for machine quilting. I've tried them, but I've never been happy with the results. Spring needles don't stabilize the fabric enough for my purposes, so I don't recommend them.

Darning Feet

During ordinary machine stitching, the feed dogs work with the presser foot to stabilize the fabric. With free-motion stitching, the feed dogs are lowered, and the fabric isn't held stable.

To increase fabric stability when free-motion stitching, use a darning foot. It has a little circle, through which the needle passes as you stitch. The circle acts as an embroidery hoop, holding the fabric taut for light free-motion straight stitching.

Learn whether your machine uses a low shank, high shank, or a clip-on foot. Bernina, Pfaff, and Viking machines have special darning feet specific to each machine. Most standard screw-on feet fit Singer and New Home machines. Some older machines, such as the old black Singers (and Featherweights particularly), work better with a darning spring.

In selecting a darning foot, the general rule is, the bigger the hole on the foot, the less stabilization it offers. For example, because it mashes everything down, the large-holed Bernina foot is wonderful for free-motion appliquéing pieces that have already been machine embroidered. But it would not be my choice for regular free-motion straight stitching.

Basting Gun

My QuilTak basting gun shoots plastic tags into quilt sandwiches, holding the layers together for quilting. The QuilTak's needle has been known to punch holes in fabric, but I don't mind, because I'm always able to stitch heavily over a hole. If you are concerned, test first. A basting gun is much easier on my hands and wrists than safety pins.

Designing in Color

COLOR THEORY

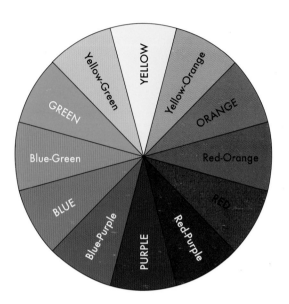

The color wheel is an excellent tool for discovering relationships between colors.

Color theory is a system used to define or dictate an artist's color choices. It's a vast subject, and far too complicated to treat in depth in this book. Colors are visual emotion and create a personal, private language. Color theory only has a little to do with the color choices I make. Choosing a color for one of my quilts is based on my emotional response. Though most of my colors fall within the range of a realistic palette, I escape into a color daydream from time to time—there are days when the sky is fuchsia.

Color is a nonverbal phenomenon. Words can only approximate a color and often fail us when we try to discuss one. Our eyes are different from others' eyes; we literally see colors differently, with distinct degrees of color awareness and even of colorblindness. There is no guarantee that we are all seeing exactly the same thing when we look at color. But there are color relationships that everyone seems to respond to; we respond to the tensions created by those color relationships.

The highest visual tension is found between complementary colors, which lie directly across from each other on the wheel. Color schemes that include complementary colors tend to be electric and wild. Colors next to each other on the wheel, analogous colors, have the least amount of tension between them. Analogous colors appear rich and blended in a work; they lend a sense of the luxurious.

Monochromatic color schemes include only one hue, or color. These palettes derive their tension through the play of tonalities (the amount of gray in a color) and values (dark and light versions of a color). Monochromatic schemes tend to be quiet, rich, and subtle.

For me, making color choices involves creating tensions and resolving them to harmony. Tension by itself is too jarring, but harmony can become boring. What I seek is balance and resolution. Bold, shocking colors are always tempting, just because they're showy. But I find that there needs to be a balance, a sense of visual rightness.

The tension produced by colors provides the tone for the whole piece. Is it to be restful? Playful? Energized? Turbulent? The fabric chosen for a piece determines that.

What resolves the tension is the action of the eye, blending the colors to a neutral shade. The artist accomplishes this by adding bits of complementary colors to make browns or by graying colors with black or tinting them with white or yellow. I begin resolving tension when I dye fabric.

HAND-DYED FABRIC

Hand-dyed fabric is the perfect surface for machine quilting, embroidery, and embellishment. Because quilting stitches show better on a single piece of hand-dyed fabric than on printed or pieced fabrics, and because hand-dyed fabric has much more life than commercial solids, I make it available to my students for purchase. If you fall in love with a hand-dyed piece, buy it. It only happens once; you won't see it again. Color combinations can be repeated, but the way the piece is folded, the way the dye drips, and a number of other factors make each piece of hand-dyed fabric unique. When you use hand-dyed fabric, the quilt starts its life as an original piece of art, before you've taken a single stitch.

Do you need to dye fabric? Maybe. All kinds of wonderful hand-dyed fabrics are available from numerous fiber artists. Most of them create work that is distinctive, their "signature"; it looks like no one else's work. If you use their dyed goods, your work may look a lot like their work.

The dyeing process certainly is not difficult. I've done it with five-year-olds. It is, however, hard on the back, and you need a strong tolerance for clutter.

There are many fine books about dyeing fabric and dyeing safety. I particularly recommend Judy Ann Walter's *Creating Color* (1989, Cooler by the Lake Productions) for someone interested the basic chemistry of dyeing. *Hand-Dyed Fabric Made Easy* by Adriene Buffington (1996, That Patchwork Place) includes valuable information about dyeing with Procion dyes, and in her book *Complex Cloth* (1996, Fiber Studio Press), Jane Dunnewold gives excellent instructions for batch dyeing. For a basic sketch of the dyeing process, the Dharma Trading Company catalog (see "Resources" on page 111) offers a short guide to fiber-reactive dyeing, and instructions come with each dye order.

Hand-dyed fabrics form the basis of my quilt environments. My method for dyeing is a cross between tie-dye and fabric painting. My methods may differ from other dyers', but the results are perfect for my quilts.

Materials for Hand Dyeing

To order the following products, refer to "Resources" on page 111.

PROCION (FIBER-REACTIVE) DYES: Unlike direct dyes, such as Rit and Cushing, Procion dye connects molecularly with natural vegetable fibers, such as cotton, rayon, and hemp. It also works beautifully with silk. Procion dye is extremely colorfast and more lightfast (resistant to fading by exposure to light) than most commercial cottons, and yields strong, rich colors.

SYNTHRAPOL: A commercial detergent, Synthrapol is formulated to be highly concentrated and to remove grease and excess dye.

WASHING SODA: Washing soda, also referred to as "dye activator" and "soda ash," is sodium carbonate, a catalyst that helps attach dye to fabric. It can be purchased at dye houses, but for years I've used the Arm and Hammer All Natural

Super Washing Soda Detergent Booster I buy at the grocery store, and I've always had excellent results.

Urea: A wetting agent that enables dye to dissolve more completely in water.

PFD (Prepared-for-Dyeing) Fabrics: Most fabrics have some type of finish or coating that resists dye or inhibits the dye process. Some finishes, like starches, can be removed by washing the fabric, but some resin coatings cannot be removed. PFD fabric has no finishes or resins. I get the best results from PFD mercerized cottons; mercerized cotton has been treated to make it more receptive to dye.

Thread Magic Formula for Hand Dyeing

Step 1: Pre-scrub

Wash the fabric in hot water with 1 teaspoon *each* of washing soda and Synthrapol. Even PFD fabrics may need to be pre-scrubbed.

Step 2: Dye soak

Soak the pre-scrubbed fabric in a solution of 1 cup of washing soda for each gallon of water. One gallon will soak 10 yards of fabric, and you can save the dye-soak water to use over and over.

Step 3: Chemical water

Mix $1/2$ cup of dried urea and 2 to 3 drops of Synthrapol into 1 quart of water. You will use small amounts of the chemical water when mixing dye.

Step 4: Dye

Mix dye powder into chemical water. For pale colors, use 1 teaspoon of dye to $1/2$ cup of chemical water. For strong and dark colors, I use 3 to 4 teaspoons of dye to $1/4$ cup of chemical water. Some Procion dye colors are stronger than others, making the amount of dye you need dependent on the color strength desired. Experiment to find what works best for you.

I usually prepare a dye palette of fifteen to twenty colors, which I place in separate containers. After presoaking the fabric in soda-ash water for 10 minutes, I apply dye with sponges while the fabric is still wet so the colors will blend and flow freely. Sometimes the best way to start dyeing a piece of fabric is to spread the cloth in a puddle of dye left over from the last piece, then sponge on more dye.

The cloth needs to cure wet, so I put it into a resealable plastic bag and let it sit for at least twenty-four hours. The way I put the fabric into the bag makes a big difference in the results. The photos at left show fabrics that were manipulated in different ways before being sealed in a bag.

Fabric that was folded and then placed in the dye bag looks different than fabric that was twisted or scrunched.

FOLDED

TWISTED

SCRUNCHED

The chemical bond of dye to fabric happens in a progression similar to radioactive decay. Most of the dye bonds within the first couple of minutes, but molecules of dye continue to bond to the fiber over a period of time. When the process of taking up the dye is complete, we say the dye has been *exhausted*. Once that has happened, the excess dye will no longer bleed onto other pieces, and it's safe to wash the dyed pieces together. I wait at least 24 hours for the fabric to cure. A longer period is better, because it allows the fabric to absorb more dye. Fabric can easily set for a week or two without harm.

When the dye is set, I remove the fabric from the plastic bags while I fill the washing machine with hot water and 1 tablespoon of Synthrapol. I add the fabric and run it through the wash-and-rinse cycle twice, adding 1 tablespoon of Synthrapol to each wash cycle. Then I line dry the fabric and run it through a mangle.

Hand-dyed fabric is a cross between an accident and a miracle. I get what I get, but I can aim for certain effects. One of the most wonderful hand-dyed effects you can create is the illusion of a light source. A light source is both a light area in the fabric and an area that seems to generate light throughout the piece. To create a light source in a piece, I dye a pale area in yellows, grays, or pastels, and then I dye darker areas in the remaining spaces. Many of my quilts appear illuminated from within by the light source dyed into the cloth.

GOLD BUG

18" x 19", ©1994.

A dyed-in-the-fabric area of yellow and gold, which darkens to maroon, suggested a light source and a flower to me. The variation in hue and value adds life and excitement to this quilt. Machine-embroidered appliqué, machine quilting, beading, and embroidery create intricate textures.

Background Fabric

The Quilt Environment

When I'm choosing fabric for a quilt, I look for a piece that creates a sense of environment, with "environment" being a flexible term. One may have a tendency to choose a natural color scheme, but who's to say what's natural? Water can be green, aqua, gray, blue, purple, or gold depending on how the light penetrates it or reflects off it.

Part of choosing a background fabric is deciding what time of day and year the quilt environment will represent. Is it noon? Twilight? Overcast? Cold or warm? Spring or summer? Foggy, rainy, or just wet? Answering these questions limits the choices I have to make.

Choosing color by season and time takes us straight back to the color wheel (page 70). Warm colors—magenta, red, orange, and yellow—are summer, fall, and noonday colors. Cool greens, aquas, blues, and violets are spring and morning colors. Muted colors indicate soft light, such as spring, dawn, or twilight. Dark, grayed, or brown colors are indicative of fall, winter, twilight, or nighttime. Pastels can be winter snows or spring blossoms.

I also decide if I want my piece to have a light source. A light source gives a piece a glow, a sense of light radiating from within. But in choosing a light source, it's wise to be aware of where it occurs in the piece and whether it is consistent with the effect you're after. Do you want bright or soft light? Diffuse or direct? In addition to using fabric with a dyed-in light source, the effect can be simulated with or enhanced by a sheer overlay.

I don't particularly make design decisions from a naturalistic viewpoint. Instead, I use imagery, colors, and fabric as metaphors for human conditions: Spring is full of beginnings, summer a time of growth and establishment, fall a time of completion, and winter a fallow time to rest and refurbish. Dawn is a time of awakening and action; night is a time of weariness and wariness; noon is a time of overwhelming heat and pressure.

Since I work in unconscious metaphors, I can't say while I'm working on a quilt that I always know why it's important that an image be in a particular setting. Often I simply have a notion that I need to follow, and I understand it much later. I'm at peace with letting myself discover the meaning of an image or a quilt after the fact. I do know that there's a sense of visual rightness that I later find has its own significance.

Pieced Backgrounds

Because of the bulk created by seam allowances, I don't like to quilt and embroider over piecing. However, I often do frame a piece of hand-dyed background fabric with a border or strip-piece two hand-dyed pieces together for a background.

When I want to give a sense of filtering light, I strip piece two hand-dyed fabrics to create that illusion. I choose one piece with a definite light source and another piece with

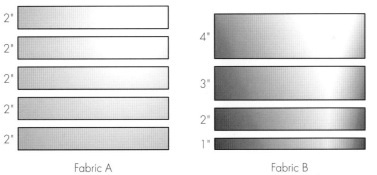

Fabric A   Fabric B

elements that both blend and contrast with the other. Sometimes I cut one piece in either 1½"- or 2"-wide strips and the other piece in a numeric progression of widths (such as 1", 2", 3", and 4" wide; or 4", 3", 2", 1", 2", 3", and 4" wide; depending on how large I want the finished quilt to be).

I place the strips horizontally in the order I cut them and then piece, alternating fabrics and using a ¼"-wide seam allowance.

The eye connects the pieced strips into one image. The alternating strips create the impression of filtered light, and often the narrowest strip becomes the horizon line.

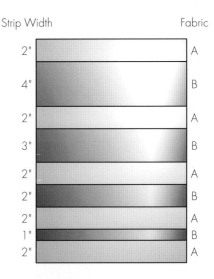

Strip Width	Fabric
2"	A
4"	B
2"	A
3"	B
2"	A
2"	B
2"	A
1"	B
2"	A

ENVY (detail)

Two "light source" fabrics, joined in strips, create a background of filtered light. (See the full quilt on page 40.)

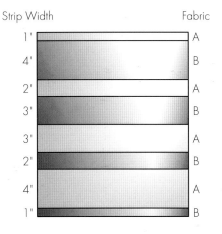

Strip Width		Fabric
1"		A
4"		B
2"		A
3"		B
3"		A
2"		B
4"		A
1"		B

Sometimes I place two equal-sized pieces together on the cutting board, and then cut them in the numeric progression described previously. I intersperse the strips in order, starting with the widest strip from one piece and the narrowest from the other. At the center, the middle-sized strips are the same width, and that makes a horizon line.

I usually don't border stripped backgrounds. A borderless piece has a soft finish that I particularly like for dreamy sky and water scenes; the images seem to float off the edges of the quilt. But I'm always free to ignore my rules when they don't work. If I put a border on a stripped piece, the main design should have a strong image so the border doesn't overpower it.

Borders give a sense of completion. They *contain* the figures within the quilt; they punctuate images. I use a border when I want to make an image appear larger and bolder or when I want a contained look. Often I use a narrow—1 1/2"- to 2"-wide—inner border in a bright or contrasting fabric to accentuate the contained effect. The larger border's color must also contrast with the quilt and the inner border, either in hue or in intensity. Particularly effective is a border that blends with the center panel at one side of the quilt and contrasts strongly at the other.

Sometimes a border is *too* confining. I like my borders best when the interior creatures break out just a little. In the quilt shown at left, the catfish swims out through the border, keeping the center square from being static.

CATFISH HEAVEN
13" x 13", ©1996.
(Collection of Rhoda M. Bombard)
The outer border blends and contrasts with the catfish and the quilt interior for an exciting interaction of values.

For small quilts, I often set a square on point. I start with a small square and sew four setting triangles of a contrasting color to it. If the center square is darker than the triangles, the lighter triangles visually expand the edges of the piece, making it look airy and open. If the square is lighter than the triangles, the darker triangles tend to contain the images in the square. Again, pulling elements in and out of the square to create a visual path lends the work excitement and spark.

THE REEF

13" x 13", ©1995.

The dark triangles around the on-point square form a dynamic background.

THREAD EFFECTS

When hand dyeing fabric, we mix dyes to achieve a desired color. Mixing embroidery threads is different because the colors never really combine. They lie next to each other and our eyes mix them for us. The effect is similar to a post-Impressionist art form called *pointillism*, in which Seurat and other artists painted with tiny dots of color. Because the colors never muddy each other in mixing, there's a richness and depth that can't be achieved any other way.

FLUTTERING

12" x 12", ©1996.

The wings and body of this hummingbird range from purples to blues and greens. The colors keep their gemlike tones because they mix only in the viewer's eyes.

Affecting Color with Stippling

TWILIGHT TIME (detail)

Because the colors are complementary, the purple stippling adds a charge to this predominately yellow background. (See the full quilt on page 23.)

Stippling is a straight stitch sewn in close, meandering rows. This stitching technique not only fills in space but also affects the background's color, tone, and value. Stippling with thread of a similar color to the background fabric softens the area. Contrasting thread colors charge a background with energy. The details on a piece of hand-dyed fabric jump off the quilt once the background has been stippled with nylon thread. Stippled monofilament nylon and metallic threads can separate background from foreground and other design elements by establishing a contrasting visual texture. Flat metallic threads make a fabulous shimmering contrast to a solid rayon or wrapped metallic thread in appliqué pieces.

Creating Contrast with Outlines

To embroider a sharp outline around a shape, we need to break the instinct (or custom) of matching thread to fabric. The line made by one thread is so thin that strong, bold contrasts and colors are essential. When outlining a design element, I use either complementary colors or opposite intensities. Bright orange thread sings against a dark blue background because the colors are complementary. Iridescent white thread would do the same, because of the value contrast. Similar shades and values, such as medium blue against dark blue, would be barely visible. Often I choose the thread that stands out the most, regardless of color.

Thick threads, such as perle cotton, perle rayon, ribbon thread, Candlelight, Madeira Glamour, and Decor work best for outlining. With them, you can create ghostlike shapes with the simple, clean line of a contour drawing.

SKINNY DIPPING (detail)

This fish pops out against the dark backdrop because of the bright yellow, orange, and purple threads in the stitching. (See the full quilt on page 36.)

Shading Appliqués

To shade an object with zigzag embroidery, you need a wide range of tones of the same hue, ranging from dark to light—I frequently use twenty to thirty colors in one large appliqué. It doesn't matter if the colors clash a little—it creates excitement. I've often used blue- and yellow-tinged greens in the same appliqué. On spools, placed together on the sewing table, they're less promising, but the contrast really adds life and energy to the finished piece. Adding a dark complementary color just inside the edges of the appliqué contributes to the shading process.

TULIP TIME (detail)

I embroidered the frog with the range of metallic, rayon, and nylon threads shown at left and then appliquéd the embroidered piece to the quilt. (See the full quilt on page 101.)

Metallic threads read lighter than rayon threads of the same color because they reflect more light. Of the metallics, wrapped threads are the least reflective, and flat threads are the most reflective.

Flat metallic threads do not blend well, so I use them almost exclusively for stippling, not for embroidered appliqué. The exception is when I embroider animal eyes. The sheen of flat metallic threads makes glittery pupils; the area is so small the thread doesn't need to blend well.

Since a twenty-color range is more difficult to find in metallic threads, I sometimes embroider with rayon and then "dust" the piece afterward with a light stitching of metallic thread. Layering threads this way works well because the metallics on top reflect light and also add texture. Stitching rayon thread over metallics tends to result in a dull and lackluster finish; I don't recommend it.

Drawing and Design

THE DIRTY "D" WORD

Almost all my quilts are small worlds with creatures in them, and the design usually starts with the creature. Here we run smack-dab into the Dirty "D" Word: *draw*. Yes, I know it has four letters, and no, I did not mean to swear at you. At some point, most of my students tell me they can't draw. I tell them the truth: I'm not secure about drawing either, but I don't let it stop me. Drawing is a skill, a muscle that can be built up, but this happens only when we exercise it. We will never do anything well until we give ourselves the grace to try, to fail, to try again, and to succeed.

Each of us has an artist inside. Most often she is full of energy, ideas, and experiments. She plays without fear of failure or need of success. Usually that person is around three to five years old. Now, the good news is that she is still there, no matter how old you are. She's just done too many dishes and filled out too many forms to be enthusiastic about anything.

So, cut her some slack. Buy her new crayons or markers. Give her special classes, a space of her own to work in, and time to play. Show off her work with pride. Let the dust rhinoceroses collect under the bed for awhile. You'll be astonished with your artist when you let her loose.

If you're still scared, start slowly by feeding your eyes. You only *think* you know what a frog looks like. Take a trip to the aquarium or to the pet store. Get pictures. Buy an animal toy and look at it from all angles.

To feed my eyes, I constantly refer to drawing sources such as these.

When we think about objects, we usually think in words. As words fail us in describing color, they also fail us in describing form. We need to see to draw. And the images are waiting everywhere.

Look for animals in art books, nature books, children's books, magazines, and coloring books. Some pictures will define a color range for your desired image. Hopefully, one will show the animal at the angle you desire.

Once I've settled on a figure or creature, I have to decide on its shape, shading, and pose, and I need to define its environment, or background.

The animal's pose needs to fit its nature. Is it sitting in dignity? Jumping wildly? In swift flight, or moving slowly through water? As you feed your eyes, look for pictures of your animal in a pose that feels right.

LEAF DANCE
12" x 12", ©1995. (Collection of Rebecca Brown)

Inspired by the photograph at left by James P. Rowan, I embroidered and then appliquéd the frog on hand-dyed cottons in greens, pinks, and oranges.

The picture you find may not show every aspect in detail, such as the texture of a fin or the placement of feathers. Don't worry. Find another source for those details. Don't let realism stand in your way. It's fun to accurately reproduce a frog's spots, but sometimes it's more fun to get carried away by a wild color or an outlandish design.

While doing research, it's wise to be aware of copyright laws. The copyright protects artists and writers from plagiarism. How do we honor a copyright? Most often, once I've drawn something from a picture, it has changed enough to take on my style and a life of its own. This is why I draw rather than trace. If, in designing a quilt, you feel a need to trace, look up art that's copyright-free. There are books full of wonderful drawings and etchings no longer under copyright, for guilt-free use. Enlarge or reduce images with a photocopy machine, or enlarge on an overhead projector. You can use one of your own photos as a source. By tracing a photo you can usually get an accurate image, but remember, tracing often lacks the spontaneity of a drawing.

THE DESIGN PLAN

I usually make two drawings when I design a quilt. The first is a shaded sketch of the animal placed in a rough sketch of its world. The second is a line drawing of the animal on a stabilizer such as Pellon's Totally Stable. I draw this version the actual finished size. Between these sketches, I have a good idea where my quilt is going. I do, however, regularly change my mind without guilt. As my quilts progress, I try to look at them frequently from a distance to see the overall effect, adjusting anything that seems out of balance.

I translated the photo on page 81 into this sketch.

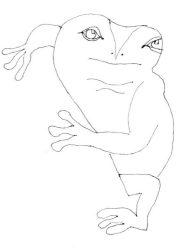

I drew this, based on the sketch, onto Totally Stable.

In my first sketch, such the one for the fish in "Twilight Pond" (page 48) shown below, I determine the animal's anatomy, pose, and shading. While shading the piece, I decide where the light is coming from and how it will reflect off the image. Is the light coming from behind? From above? From beneath? From the side? This sketch helps me to decide what tones I will later use in the embroidered appliqué.

Once I've developed the major figure, I work on its environment. Here I've sketched the design for the fishes' pond.

I construct a visual path that leads the viewer into the quilt, to the main figure, around the surface of the quilt, and finally out of the quilt. In the sketch shown at right of "Leaf Dance" (page 81), placement of the plants and novelty yarn leads the viewer's eye around the surface of the quilt. In other quilts, I've used flowers, insects, and air and water currents to create pathways. The visual path can take any shape, but simple spirals and swirls are most effective. On the quilt top, accentuate and define the pathway with quilting, layers of organza and tulle, or couched novelty yarns.

Different quilts need different amounts of planning. I draw enough to understand where I'm going. Some sketches are more complete than others.

In this sketch for "Twilight Time" (page 23), I added detail to the bugs but not to the environment.

In this sketch for "The Problem with Princes" (page 31), I included details for the environment as well as for the frog.

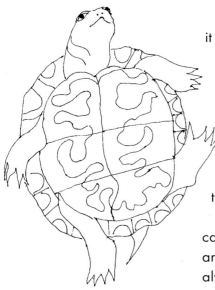

Because this turtle will be embroidered from the back, I draw a mirror image of the design onto stabilizer.

Shown at left is a line drawing of a turtle, which I drew to the finished size it would be in the quilt. At this stage, I include all the legs, arms, and antennae, if any, even if they are too thin for appliqué. Since I stitch over a drawing when embroidering, and because I stitch from the back of the piece, I draw a mirror image of the design onto Totally Stable. Next, I iron the Totally Stable onto a base fabric. Once I've outline stitched the shape (ignoring the smaller parts), I carefully remove the unstitched segment of the stabilizer and iron it onto the back of the quilt, behind the spot where the finished appliqué will be. I later use the stabilizer as a guide for embroidering the smaller parts directly onto the quilt top.

A number of small creatures surrounding and interacting with a larger one can animate a design. As an exercise, I draw a quantity of frogs, birds, bugs, and fish onto Totally Stable for later use. I keep the sketches in a bag so I'll always have something handy for filling in quilts.

Making a quilt is like raising a child. You may want your child to be a doctor or a librarian, but she may have a serious interest in working with motorbikes. At some point in the quiltmaking process, I lose control, and like a child, the quilt develops its own life. This phenomenon is true for any creative process. It happens with all my quilts, and I hope it will happen with yours too. It's magical.

Embroidering with a Machine

For machine embroidery, the magic is in the threads you choose. You can use almost any kind of embroidery thread. Nothing is too fragile, too thick, or too lumpy. The secret lies in knowing when to use a particular thread in the bobbin and how to use the bobbin case.

Almost all difficult threads are tame as kittens when wound in the bobbin. Metallic threads, thick threads, and flat metallic threads all behave perfectly when stitched from the back of the quilt. Why? Every time the thread goes into the fabric from the top, it's already gone through your needle at least fifty times, back and forth, just like a little saw. *Of course* the thread breaks. Bobbin thread is picked up only once by the top thread as the hook of the machine wraps it around, which is much easier on the thread.

With machine stitching, both sides of the fabric show the work equally. I often switch sides, working from the front or back depending on the threads.

Since my commercial machine requires polyester embroidery thread, and since those threads don't come in a wide range of colors, I choose one shade of polyester for the top and a range of related colors for the bobbin. For example, if I were embroidering an area from the back of the quilt, I might use one shade of yellow polyester thread in the top and three or four shades of gold metallic thread in the bobbin. The yellow polyester is close enough in hue to the metallics that if a little shows through it won't affect the color.

I don't use specialized bobbin thread (thread originally intended for use in the bobbin for lingerie and machine embroidery). No matter how well I've adjusted the tension, bits of it show through.

Different machines like different threads better than others, and personal preferences differ as well, but the threads listed below are ones that work for me. To learn more, refer to "Threads" on page 62.

How to Use Embroidery Thread

Embroidery weight (#30 or #40) cottons, polyesters, and rayons work in both the top of the sewing machine and in the bobbin. I tend to prefer rayons because I'm a magpie and I love their sheen.

Good brands of cotton embroidery thread include Mettler Metrosene and DMC. Good brands of rayon thread include Alcazare, Madeira, Sulky, Anton Robinson, and Venus. Madeira makes Neon, a fine polyester embroidery thread.

Another wonderfully useful thread is monofilament nylon. I use it for basic quilting and for couching threads. I also use it for the final topstitching on bias binding. This thread is not related to the monofilament nylon of the past. It's fine as a hair and will not harm your machine.

NOTE: *All threads used in the top of the machine can be strengthened with Sewer's Aid. This is a liquid silicone treatment you can apply directly to the thread while it is still on the spool. It doesn't permanently change the thread color and the thread is much stronger afterward. I highly recommend it.*

How to Use Metallic Thread

Metallic threads are more fragile than embroidery threads. For easiest use, I wind them in the bobbin. I have, however, had luck using metallic-flecked threads in both the top and in the bobbin, particularly when I treat them first with Sewer's Aid and use a topstitching needle. I've used the following brands of metallic thread in both the top and bobbin with ease: Madeira Super Twist metallic, Alcazare metallic, Kreinikord, and Coats and Clark metallics.

I've found the following threads too thick to use in the top of the machine; they do work well in the bobbin with an adjusted or bypassed bobbin case (see page 67): Madeira Glamour, Madeira Decor, Madeira Lamé, YLI Candlelight, YLI Perle Rayon, #5 and #8 perle cotton, rayon ribbon thread, and metallic ribbon thread.

The following threads are too fragile for use in the top of the machine. They work well when wound in a regular bobbin case: YLI Single Ply metallic; Madeira FS metallic; Sulky metallic; Sulky Sliver; Stream Lamé Tinsel, Madeira Jewel prismatic thread; Gutterman metallic, Kreinik blending filament, Kreinik high-luster blending filament, and Kanagawa metallic.

HOW TO USE NOVELTY YARN

Lumpy or bumpy threads won't fit through the opening of a bobbin case, but you still can use them with wonderful results. Couch them to the top of the quilt with monofilament nylon—threaded in both the top and in the bobbin—using a zigzag or fagoting stitch

I like Madeira Estaz; Madeira Radiance, and other novelty yarns such as chenille, bouclé, and variegated, textured, and multifiber yarns.

Don't be afraid to experiment. Investigation is part of the process. When I find a new thread I want to try, I make a practice piece to see what it will do. Keep note of the threads that work best for you and for your machine.

EMBROIDERY STITCHES

The Garnet Stitch

To make a garnet stitch, just move the fabric in circles under the needle. It's a simple stitch, but the applications are varied and wonderful. Refer to "Stitching in Free-Motion" on page 100 for more information.

↝ Done in a straight stitch or a zigzag, loosely or tightly, the garnet stitch makes a great stipple (see page 102). A loose, flowing straight-stitched garnet stitch creates leaves for the trees in the quilt shown at left.

MISTY MORNING
11" x 15", ©1996.
(Collection of Marie J. Geary)

❧ To shade an object, lay one color of garnet stitch on top of and next to another color, and then repeat with other colors. I shaded this elephant with layers of loose zigzag garnet stitching.

FOR VERENA REGINA
14" x 15", ©1996.
(Collection of Verena Rybicki)

❧ Worked with thick thread and in a straight stitch, the garnet stitch makes wonderful scales and fins. For the alligator's scales, I used a straight-stitched garnet stitch in thick perle cotton and Madeira Decor rayon thread.

LIVING ON THE EDGE (detail)

(See the full quilt on page 34.)

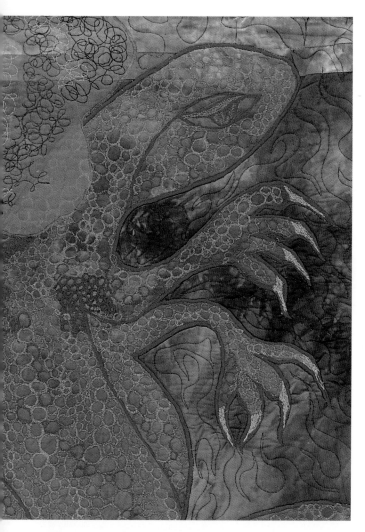

↬ Done in tight circles with a zigzag stitch, the garnet stitch creates marvelous texture. A tight zigzag garnet stitch makes pebbly lizard skin.

LIVING LAVA (detail)

(See the full quilt on page 16.)

The Zigzag Stitch

The zigzag stitch is incredibly versatile. It can be done either with free-motion techniques or with the feed dogs engaged. I prefer free-motion zigzag stitching because it offers more variety. I can control the angle of the fabric as it goes through the machine, and different angles of approach produce very different stitches. You can zigzag stitch in straight rows, from side to side, and at an angle. I did all the stitches shown at left with the same machine setting.

STRAIGHT ZIGZAG LINES: Fabric moved straight through the machine produces a wide, solid, straight line. It looks like a standard satin stitch, but I control the density of the stitching by how fast I move the fabric. A straight line of close zigzag stitching is thick and striking. I use it to create bold, decisive lines, to make buildings or walls, and to mark strong divisions within a piece.

SLANTED ZIGZAG LINES: Moving fabric through the machine at an angle creates a slanted zigzag, a thinner line like a stem stitch, perfect for outlining an appliqué. All my embroidered appliqués start out drawn in a slanted zigzag. It's also the perfect appliqué stitch; it covers well for a smooth, solid look.

SIDE-TO-SIDE-ZIGZAG LINES: Moving the fabric from side to side produces a layered stitch, which I use to fill in areas. Instead of looking like a line of stitching, a row of side-to-side zigzag stitches looks like the thread was laid strand by strand, one on top of another. I create rich, elegant fills with this stitch by layering colors one at a time. The side-to-side zigzag allows me to subtly change colors and values to achieve the perfect effect.

Controlling Distortion

A zigzag stitch, by its nature, is bound to cause distortion. As you stitch, the sewing thread grabs a yarn of the fabric, then reaches over several other yarns to grab another. Because the sewing thread is under tension, the stitches can pull the fabric's yarns together, causing them to bunch. These distortions seem small at first, but by the time a design is complete, the quilt may be out of shape and ruffled. To control zigzag distortion, do all zigzag embroidery in a hoop, even when using a darning foot. Choose a thin wooden hoop that tightens with a screwdriver. I find a 9"- to 12"-diameter hoop works best—the larger the hoop, the less support it gives. Sewing-machine stores and fabric centers carry hoops.

If the embroidered image is less than 2" x 2", you can embroider it directly onto the quilt top. Use a stabilizer under the top, a hoop, and a 1/4"-wide zigzag stitch to prevent distortion. If the image is larger than 2" x 2", make an appliqué.

EARLY BIRD
14" x 15", ©1995.
(Collection of Donna Hinman)

I embroidered the worm directly onto the quilt top. Because it is smaller than 2" x 2", and because I used a narrow zigzag stitch, distortion was minimal. For the appliqué and quilting, I used rayon, metallic, and monofilament nylon threads, in addition to novelty yarn.

EMBROIDERED APPLIQUÉS

Small images are intimate and fun, but big pictures are the real thrill for me. I love a large figure that looks everyone in the eye. Creating these large images presents certain logistical problems. Large pieces embroidered onto cloth can ruffle at the edge like a child's party dress. The answer is to set up the work so the ruffled edge gets eliminated in the process of production.

I work heavily embroidered pieces on a separate cloth with stabilizer behind it. After I've finished the embroidery, I appliqué the piece to the quilt with a straight stitch. Though the edges ruffle and pull and make a mess, once the piece has been appliquéd to the quilt the edges can be trimmed with appliqué scissors. After trimming, I encase the raw edges with a free-motion slanted zigzag stitch.

Embroidery stitched directly onto the quilt top produces a very different look from embroidered appliqué, as shown in the quilt below.

ARMADILLO SUNSET
34" x 30", ©1995.

The butterfly at the upper left is an embroidered appliqué, and the one at its right was embroidered directly onto the quilt top. The appliquéd butterfly is slightly raised, while the embroidered one recedes, adding dimension. For the embroidery, I chose rayon, metallic, iridescent, and monofilament nylon threads.

Background Fabric

As a base for embroidery, I either use the same fabric the piece will be appliquéd to, or I choose a color that blends with the embroidery threads. With white and black fabrics, unsightly bits of the background show through where the embroidery doesn't completely cover the fabric. Don't be fooled into thinking a white or black background won't show. It will.

Mechanical Details

Use a size 80 or size 90 topstitching needle or a denim needle for embroidery. If the fabric is tightly woven it might tear; if it does, try a smaller needle.

When embroidering appliqués with free-motion stitching, use a darning foot on the machine. Use an open-toe darning foot when stitching over previously sewn threads. The open toe is less likely to catch the other stitching. A darning foot with a large ring works best for stitching down the appliqué, "mashing" the appliqué to make the stitching easier.

Shaded Appliqués

When shading appliqués, it helps to determine where the light source is in relation to the figure. I refer to the shaded drawing I made of the design (see "The Design Plan" on pages 82–84) to decide where the appliqué belongs and where the light source is.

I draw two lines on the sketch to mark the boundaries of the light source. Where is the light falling? On which side of the appliqué is it strongest? I then divide the appliqué into three value areas: dark, medium, and light.

This is the black-and-white sketch for "Secret Garden," which is shown on page 52.

I used the sketch shown at left to determine the shading of the lobsters in the final piece.

NOTE: *Because the zigzag stitch draws up the fabric a little across the width of the stitches, each line slightly shrinks the image. When rows of zigzag stitches cover a quilt, an image's finished size is reduced by five to ten percent. Plan for distortion by deciding in which direction the majority of the zigzag rows will lie, and correct for shrinkage by drawing the image a little wider.*

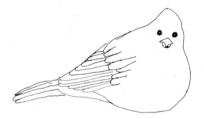

The "Nesting Confusion" sketch is reversed from and wider than the image in the finished quilt.

I draw a reversed version of the desired image onto stabilizer. My favorite stabilizer for drawing is Totally Stable from Sulky: it's a good surface for sketching, irons onto fabric like freezer paper, and tears away completely when I'm done stitching. I iron the stabilizer onto the back of the quilt top or onto the back of the fabric I'm working on.

NESTING CONFUSION

13" x 13", ©1996. (Collection of Martha Brooks)

I used rayon, metallic, and monofilament nylon threads, with novelty yarn and thread scraps for the nest.

I put the piece in a hoop and stretch the surface drum tight, and then I outline the image with a slanted-zigzag stem stitch in the darkest thread. I prefer to use a black-flecked metallic for this.

With the darkest color, I stitch the darkest areas of the appliqué, just outside the outline. I first establish the color edge with a line of straight zigzag stitching, and then I move the fabric in a side-to-side zigzag to make a feathered edge inside the appliqué.

I layer each color over the last in the same way. I use the three or four darkest colors in the dark areas only. Next, I stitch the darkest medium color over the dark area that moves into the medium area, and then layer medium colors, repeating the process I used for the dark area. I repeat the process for the light-value areas, finishing with the lightest value.

To determine the value of thread, it helps to look at it through red glass or red cellophane. Metallic threads will always register lighter than they are because they're reflective. I wait to stitch the delicate bits—anything less than 1/2" wide—until I'm appliquéing the piece to the quilt top.

I iron the appliqué after every two or three rows of stitching. It's time to iron when the embroidery won't lie flat in the hoop. I use a steam iron and stretch the piece, ignoring the ruffled edge of the background fabric, which I will trim later.

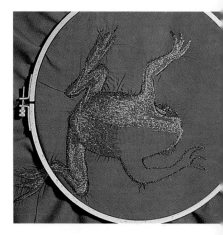

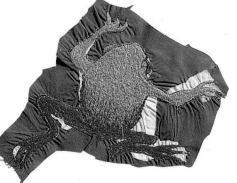

Three-Dimensional Appliqué

and Machine-Made Lace

By extending just a little the techniques I've already covered, you can make both three-dimensional figures and machine-made needlelace. Instead of embroidering onto fabric, I embroider onto a sandwich made up of two layers of nylon tulle and two layers of Solvy stabilizer. The stitching techniques are the same as for embroidered appliqué. When the piece is finished, I trim away the net and the Solvy. A solidly embroidered image will appear to be made of nothing but thread and will be finished on both sides.

MOONRISE 2

13" x 12", ©1996. (Collection of Katherine and Ninon Gallagher)

I embroidered the moth with rayon threads and finished the wings with an iridescent metallic border. To appliqué it to the quilt, I stitched through the body.

If bits of net show when the embroidery is complete, the piece has the appearance of lace. I made the leaf shown below from nylon net, Solvy, metallic thread, and Totally Stable. I made a sandwich of two layers of Solvy, two layers of net, and the image drawn on Totally Stable. I straight-stitched the leaf and then used a tight zigzag to make the heavy lines. After removing the Totally Stable, I stitched the lightweight lines.

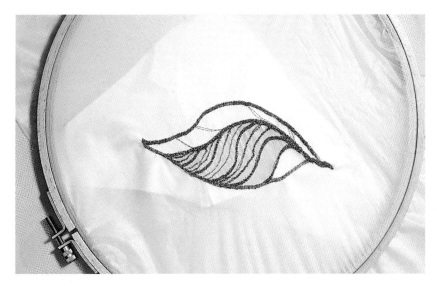

The major difference between stitching embroidery and making lace is that the Totally Stable needs to be pulled out once the major lines have been sewn. The detail stitching is done on just the net and the Solvy.

I cut away the excess stabilizer and net, and edged the leaf with a buttonhole stitch over gimp.

To finish, I rinsed the piece in water, leaving only the stitching and the net.

To stitch over the gimp or light cotton cord around the edge of the needlelace piece, I choose the same tight, narrow zigzag I'd use for a buttonhole on woven cotton. I use a buttonhole foot with two channels (or thread escapes) on the bottom of the foot. These channels allow the stitches to pass under the foot easily. Engage the feed dogs, and stitch around the edge of the appliqué, running the stitches through the left channel. It's a perfect finish.

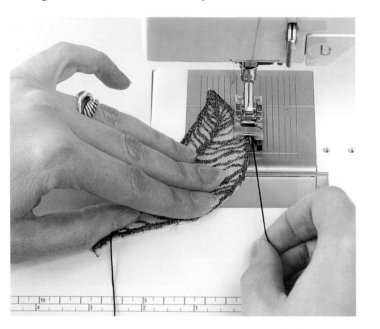

Channels
or
thread escapes

Put the lace in water to dissolve the Solvy. After the stabilizer has dissolved, place the lace between two towels to dry. Once the lace is dry, steam press it, using a pressing cloth. Stitch the lace in place directly on the quilt top. In the quilt shown at right, I embroidered the hummingbird wings with black and silver metallic threads onto a light glitter tulle and then finished with black metallic thread over gimp. I turned under the raw edges of the wings and tail when appliquéing the piece in place.

NOTE: *If you stitch inside the edges of the lace, both the edges and the lace will remain three-dimensional.*

FLITTERING
12" x 12", ©1996.

Making Sheer Magic

Set your appliqués and lace aside while you prepare your background and other elements for your quilt. I create that background with hand-dyed fabric, which I embellish in several ways with appliqués made from cottons and sheers.

CUTAWAY APPLIQUÉ

Most appliqués are small pieces, fused or stitched to the quilt. Cutaway appliqué allows me to create large images with less distortion. I use this technique with both sheer and opaque fabrics, for different effects. Opaque hand-dyed cottons make solid images or a heavy-lined look. Sheers lend themselves to diverse natural appearances, including sunlight, shadow, flame, water, mist, and fog. Organza, tulle, and net—in both synthetic and natural fibers—work well.

I've found that the more I move fabric around once it's cut into shapes, the more likely it is to stretch. Conversely, if I lay an appliqué fabric on the quilt top, stitch the shape I want, and then cut away the excess, the fabric is less likely to stretch. This method works best when I want a soft look. Over the quilt top and stabilizer I place the layer or layers of appliqué fabric. I smooth the layers flat, and then baste them together with pins or QuilTaks. Referring to the drawing I made of the visual path (page 83), I draw the appliqué's outline onto the top layer with chalk. With a darning foot on the machine, I stitch over the chalked line with a straight stitch in either rayon or monofilament thread. When I've finished stitching, I cut away the fabric outside the stitching lines.

ESCAPING DAWN
20" x 18", ©1992.
(Collection of Clarion Ferrono)

I created the fluid bat wings and air currents with cutaway appliqué. Solid free-motion zigzag in black rayon thread finishes the edges. I cutaway-appliquéd with black cotton on a background of mauve-and-yellow–green hand-dyed cotton. I stitched details in metallic and rayon threads.

FUSED APPLIQUÉS

There are times when fusing an appliqué to your top is better than stitching it in place. A fused piece has a firm line that won't shift while you stitch. I fuse moons and suns, leaves and corals—any small shape that might easily stretch when stitched. Organza and cotton are easy to fuse. If you use a pressing cloth, you can even fuse net.

I prefer Aleene's fusible web because the coating of fusible glue is dense, and the paper backing keeps the glue off the iron. If you've had ugly experiences with iron-on fusible webs without paper backings, put them in the past. This product is much nicer.

I set my iron to steam and as hot as the fabric will permit. It's wise to test a scrap first. I cut a piece of fusible web that is slightly larger than the appliqué shape. (I draw

SUNSET 1

10" x 10", ©1996. (Collection of Charlene Lohmeire)

I fused the sun directly to the background to prevent the edges from fraying and catching when I stippled the quilt. I used cutaway appliqué for the tulle overlays because it was easier to cut the fabric after stitching than it would have been to stitch over delicate edges that might have stretched out of shape.

the shape on the paper backing if I'm concerned about it, keeping in mind that what I draw will be reversed.) I fuse the web in place, glue side next to the fabric, following the manufacturer's directions. I let the fused piece cool a minute, and then I trim it. You can trim with the paper backing still on the fabric or you can remove it first; removing the paper spares the scissors from being dulled.

I set the appliqué on the quilt top, glue-side down. Following the manufacturer's directions, I fuse the appliqué in place. Later, I'll need to stabilize the bond with some kind of stitching, but it will hold until I do.

I fuse net and tulle as well as cotton and organza, being careful to use a Teflon ironing cloth or a piece of the web's backing paper as a pressing cloth to keep glue off the iron. Afterward, I lay a white cotton cloth over the appliqué and press it to remove any excess glue. I remove the white cloth while it's still hot. I repeat this process until the excess glue is gone.

Each time you press, use a different place on the cotton press cloth, or the glue residue will transfer to your top.

ENCASED EDGES

The edges of appliqués are not stable enough to be left on their own after being trimmed. They need to be stitched down in some way. Different threads and methods give different results. Some sheers require more care and more protection than others.

MOON IN THE MIST

25" x 33", ©1992.
(Collection of Clarion Ferrono)

I finished the organza layers with a honey-comb stitch worked in monofilament nylon thread. The honeycomb stitch keeps the organza from fraying.

Rayon, polyester, cotton, and YLI Wonder thread (monofilament nylon) are all good choices for edge stitching. Whatever thread you use needs to be embroidery weight; regular sewing thread is just too lumpy for these applications. For most stitching, an appliqué foot and raised feed dogs work best.

A zigzag stitch is a good choice for straight lines or for areas where you want a minimal amount of stitching. A zigzag stitch of monofilament nylon thread is nearly invisible; a blind-hem stitch around the edge of the appliqué looks almost like hand appliqué. When following difficult curves or sharp angles, I suggest lowering the feed dogs and using a zigzag stitch. Stabilize edges by straight stitching back and forth over them, perpendicular to the edges. This stabilizing stitch is flashy in rayons and metallics, subtler in monofilament nylon thread.

Stitching worked in rayon or cotton thread creates a solid line. Choose a color that either blends into the background or accentuates the appliqué. Flecked metallic threads produce a showy effect, and smoky monofilament nylon thread creates an almost invisible line on sheers.

For organzas, particularly iridescent ones, stitch densely, because they fray quite easily. Tulles, because they don't fray, do very well with a honeycomb stitch in monofilament nylon thread. This stitch catches the net effectively and unobtrusively. To make the honeycomb stitch, I use a walking foot, with the feed dogs raised. Computer novelty stitches are also worth a try. Experiment to see what works best.

Applying Embroidered Appliqués

Once an appliqué is completely filled in with embroidery, it can be stitched in place. I trim the extra fabric from the edges of the piece, leaving approximately 1/2"; then I fasten the appliqué onto the prepared quilt sandwich with pins or QuilTaks. I place a large-ringed darning foot on the machine, and, using a free-motion straight stitch, I stitch around the edges of the appliqué.

NOTE: *I use appliqué, or pelican, scissors to trim away the excess fabric. Appliqué scissors have one narrow blade and one wide one. The wide "bill" keeps me from cutting into the appliqué.*

If there is a puckering disaster, I cure it by cutting along one or more of the design lines in the affected area until the piece lies flat. When I stitch the appliqué to the background, I fill in the empty area and join the cut edges with a slanted zigzag. After it's all been stitched down, no one can tell the piece was ever cut.

Using rayon, flecked metallic, or black Madeira Super Twist thread, I work from the top side, covering the edges of the appliqué with a free-motion slanted zigzag stitch. I add details like legs, antennae, and tendrils at this time as well.

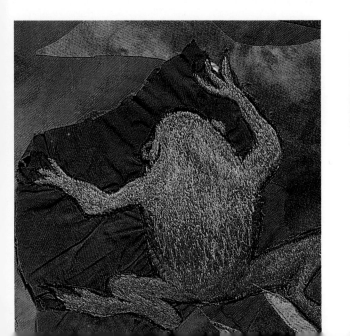

Stitching in Free-Motion

GARNET STITCHING

STIPPLING

CONTOUR DRAWING

SIGNATURE

STIPPLING

Free-motion machine work is a vital element of Thread Magic quilts. In classes, I have my students practice a number of free-motion stitches. They stitch a contour "drawing" of an object, stipple quilt different patterns, garnet stitch (stitching around and around in continuous circles) several designs, and stitch their signatures. It takes a while before the stitches are even, but practice develops the ability to stitch in any direction and to make beautifully fluid lines.

CONTOUR DRAWING

To make a contour drawing, the artist looks directly at the subject while working, not at the work in progress. The trick is to never lift the pencil until the drawing is done. This last step—not stopping until you're finished—is the key to contour drawing with the machine. The machine stitch creates one unbroken line that is, like contour drawings in pencil, full of spontaneity and life.

To begin, I stitch a basic outline of the animal or plant. Because I use a straight stitch, a thick thread makes a bold line with high visual impact.

NESTLINGS
18" x 22", ©1991.
(Collection of Susan Hecker)

"Nestlings" illustrates nearly all the straight-stitch techniques. I did the basic stitching by winding thick threads in the bobbin case and sewing from the back of the quilt.

I fill in the outline with rhythmic stippling. I shade objects by changing the thread colors or values, moving from either lightest to darkest or from darkest to lightest. The last color used will be the most dominant.

NESTLINGS (detail)

I outlined the baby owls in brown perle cotton and filled in by stippling with cream perle cotton. The rim around the eyes is a straight line of garnet stitching in ecru ribbon thread. For the eyes, I used shades of brown and black. (See the full quilt on the opposite page.)

As a final touch, I gathered the contents of my thread-clipping bag to fashion a nest for the owls. I placed the nest threads on the quilt, and then pin-basted a layer of Solvy water-soluble stabilizer over it. With monofilament nylon in the top and bobbin of the machine (and using a regular bobbin case), I stippled large circles over the stabilizer, firmly attaching the loose threads to the quilt. After I finished stitching, I sprayed the piece with water until the Solvy dissolved.

Because straight stitching doesn't cause much distortion, I sometimes work on the quilt sandwich: top, stabilizer, batting, and backing. If the fabric has a light source that I want to emphasize, I draw the stitching design on the quilt top and stitch the outlines of the main portions with #40-weight rayon thread in the top and bobbin. After outlining, I turn the piece over. I wind thick thread in a second, tension-adjusted bobbin case, and then, on the back of the quilt top, stitch over the outlined image, filling in the details.

If there isn't a light source in the design, I draw the design on the back of the sandwiched quilt and then stitch the entire design from the back. If I match the color of my rayon thread to the thicker threads, the finished quilt is reversible.

I stipple over background areas of tulle and organza, usually with different shades of flat metallic thread. (See "Stippling" on page 102.) I start with a light color at the light source and then move out in progressively darker shades.

Once the details on the quilt top are complete, I embellish the visual path with novelty yarn couched in monofilament nylon. For couching, I prefer the fagoting stitch, although a simple zigzag also works.

TULIP TIME

13" x 13", ©1996.
(Collection of Loraine Campion)

A bouclé novelty yarn echoes the path of the tulips and emphasizes the frog.

STIPPLING

I use stippling, meandering patterns of stitchery, to fill in images and open areas. I tend to stipple with flat metallic threads, and because of their fragility, I always use these threads in the bobbin. I also love to stipple with monofilament nylon thread because it adds texture without covering the beautiful hand-dyed fabric underneath.

There are many kinds of stippling: it's the natural doodling of machine quilting. Stippling is most effective when it doesn't cross over itself (unless you use the garnet stitch described on pages 86–88). The stitching can move up and down, from side to side, in little curvy paths, or in big sweeping arcs. Experiment. Stippling is utterly personal, almost a signature. Try everything, and you'll find your favorite styles. For examples of stippling, see the photo at the top of page 100.

SIGNATURES

Signing one's work is essential to quiltmaking. I am offended by the whole notion of artists, particularly women, being anonymous. Making a personal statement is critical to art's process. Making that statement without signing it is a bit like writing ransom notes to the universe. I always sign and date my work, and I insist that my students sign theirs. If the art critics don't want to know who did the work, your grandchildren will.

I find that when I stitch my name in thread, it closely resembles my handwritten signature. Practice stitching your signature, making one letter flow to the next. It may take some planning and maneuvering, but once you find a way that works for you, it becomes habit. If you use rayon thread, or a flecked metallic, you can thread the top of the machine and sign left to right, just like regular handwriting.

I most often add my signature to an area stippled with flat metallic thread. I stitch my name in the same kind of thread, and because it must be wound on the bobbin, I work from the back. To do this, I've learned to stitch my name backwards. It takes practice, but it works—my being dyslexic may help!

Embellishing the Quilt Top

Once the background is created and the images are appliquéd, it's time to embellish. It's at this point, before I layer and quilt, that I embroider details and add beading.

STITCHED DETAILS

I start by working on any appliquéd reeds, leaves, or other large images that support the main images. I define these pieces either with thick threads stitched over the appliqué or with slanted zigzag stitching. After defining edges, I concentrate on interior details. To add texture to tree bark, I might stipple layers of perle cotton in several shades of brown, green, and gray. For a leaf, I might mark veins with several rows of slanted zigzag stitching.

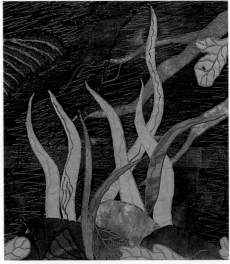

THE PROBLEM WITH PRINCES (detail)

I defined the leaves by stitching rows of perle cotton and rayon side by side. (See the full quilt on page 31.)

SCHOOLING (detail)

I emphasized the reeds with free-motion zigzag stitching near the stems. (See the full quilt on page 47.)

After embellishing the large supporting images, I add any small animal appliqués measuring less than 2" x 2". After drawing the animals on Totally Stable, I iron the stabilizer in place, directly onto the interfacing on the back of the quilt top. I embroider from the back, using a hoop and usually a straight stitch or a narrow zigzag. I shade small pieces the same way I do larger embroideries. For more information, refer to "Shaded Appliqués" on pages 91–93.

MACHINE BEADING

I occasionally bead a quilt by machine. For the best results, use a hoop and a "naked" needle (one without a presser foot). Start by dropping your feed dogs. With monofilament thread in the top and bobbin, take two or three straight stitches to anchor the stitching. Place the bead and then stitch directly into the bead hole several times. Bring the needle out and insert it in the fabric where you took the first stitches. Several more stitches in this spot secures the bead to the fabric. If done correctly, the bead pops right up.

① Take two or three stitches.

② Take several stitches.

③ Stitch over original stitches.

④ Bead turns over stitching.

GOLDBUG (detail)

For the flower stamens, I couched novelty yarn with monofilament nylon and then dotted the yarn with iridescent purple crow beads. I prefer crow beads because their size is perfect for the surface textures of my quilts, and the thickness of the needle. (See the full quilt on page 73.)

Building the Perfect Quilt Sandwich

When I began machine quilting, I did all my stitching directly on a sandwich consisting of a quilt top, a batting, and a backing. Being a creature of habit and starting out as a quilter, I thought *all* the stitching had to go through all three layers. As long as I quilted with a straight stitch, it worked pretty well. In fact, it resulted in some quilt backs that were just as fabulous as the fronts.

When I branched into zigzag embroidery, I started having more trouble getting my quilts to lie flat. I counteracted that problem with the methods you'll find in "Rehabilitating Troubled Quilts" on pages 107–109. I steamed quilts; I added a layer of nonwoven interfacing; I gathered "ruffled" quilts into borders.

As the embroidery became more intensive, so did the distortions. I loved the embroidery showing on the front and backs of my quilts. (Often, I planned a night and day side for a quilt.) But quilts that don't lie flat are completely unacceptable for competition, so I "rebacked" lumpy quilts. I taped another backing fabric to a table, lay down another layer of nonwoven interfacing, and then placed my lumpy quilt on top. I tacked through all the layers and quilted them minimally with monofilament nylon. The quilts were very heavy, but mostly flat.

The extra step of rebacking began to feel silly. As an experiment, I embroidered a series of small quilts on nonwoven interfacing only. I used a hoop whenever I zigzagged, and then backed the quilt as I would have an ordinary top, with batting between the layers. I then quilted over the main outlines with smoky monofilament nylon. I've never gone back.

I quilt a "sandwich" when I'm using only straight stitching, or when reversibility is important, such as for a jacket or for a quilt that will be used as a room divider.

FLAME TREE JACKET

©1991. (Collection of Leslie Stewart Hickland)

For this jacket, I used hand-dyed and commercial cotton fabrics. I machine quilted and embroidered with flecked metallics, perle cotton, perle rayon, Madeira Decor, and ribbon threads.

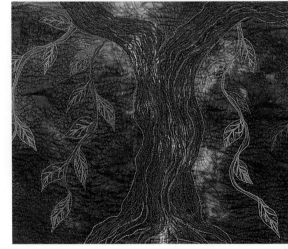

The flame side of this jacket reverses for quieter, greener moments.

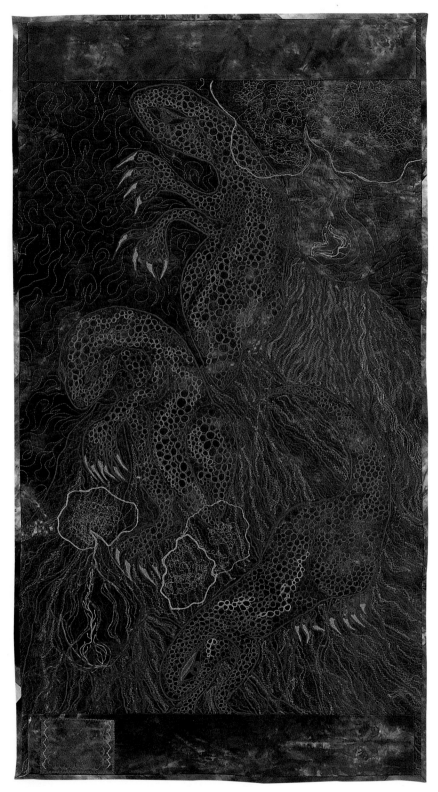

To prepare a small top for embroidery or to back a finished top, I place the top on a piece of nonwoven interfacing and baste the layers together with a QuilTak. For pieces larger than my sewing machine table, I fuse a piece of nonwoven interfacing to the top.

For a quilt with strictly straight-stitch embroidery, I prepare a regular quilt sandwich. For quilts that fit my table, I tape the quilt back, wrong side up, to the table with 1 1/2"-wide masking tape. Starting at the center of each side, I tape opposite sides, stretching the backing taut and working toward each corner. I lay the batting on top of the backing, add a layer of nonwoven interfacing, and then lay the top in place, right side up. I tack the layers of the quilt together in a 4" grid. When the basting is done, I remove the tape.

For larger quilts, I tape half the backing to the table and then layer half the quilt on top of it. I anchor the center of the quilt to the edge of the table with large binder clamps. After I tack the quilt half, I remove the masking tape, slide the remaining half of the quilt onto the table, and repeat the process.

LIVING LAVA (back of quilt)

(See the quilt front on page 16.)

Quilting with Free-Motion Techniques

I quilt my finished pieces with free-motion straight stitching in monofilament nylon thread. To start, put a darning foot on the machine and lower the feed dogs. Place both hands flat on the quilt on either side of, and close to, the needle. Exerting gentle pressure, move and rotate the fabric under the needle. The faster the machine runs, the smaller the stitches will be. The faster your hands move, the longer the stitches will be. Something in-between is best on both counts.

Rehabilitating Troubled Quilts

I hope the techniques I've discussed in this book will keep you from ever needing to do something desperate to make a quilt lie flat. But I've had my share of disasters, and in case you should have one as well, I'll share some cures with you.

There is a natural assumption that if one starts sewing squares together and puts rectangular strips around them, the quilt will have square, 90° corners. Well, it's a nice theory. Unfortunately, quiltmaking doesn't always work that way, particularly with heavily machine-stitched work. The fabric quilters use is usually woven from two sets of yarns that start out perpendicular to each other. Extra threads, as they are stitched through the fabric, push the yarns out of place. Soon, so many threads are displaced by the dense stitching that the piece distorts. Even if the quilt started out perfectly square, it may not finish that way. Usually batting and backing hang out around the sides and the quilt top's edges are uneven. If a quilt is not lying flat, try the methods described below.

NOTE: *Some metallic threads lose color when heated. Be sure to use a pressing cloth with these finishing techniques.*

STEAMING

The first step is to open up those fibers in the hope that they will make room for each other. Applying pressurized steam with a professional iron is a real help. Totally steaming the piece while adding pressure from the iron helps even out the distortion. Regular steaming throughout the quiltmaking process helps enormously.

Sometimes steaming is not enough. If that's so, consider blocking.

BLOCKING

Pin the quilt, right side out, to a backing that can take heat and steam without melting, such as cardboard, wool carpet, or Celotex. Pin along all the edges of the quilt. Push the pins all the way into the backing.

Layer a piece of thin muslin or cheesecloth over the quilt to protect it against scorching. Whatever you use should be colorless, so that it will not bleed onto the quilt. Thoroughly wet down the cloth.

Apply a very hot iron to the press cloth. The quilt doesn't need to be ironed completely dry, but let it air dry before you remove the pins. Letting it dry overnight in a well-ventilated room and then binding it in the morning works well.

Even after blocking, it's unlikely that the quilt will be perfectly square. Just remember: don't get mad, get even.

GETTING EVEN

Each quilt loses at least $1/4$" around each edge, under the binding. Most quilters design that $1/4$" into their quilt tops. If we design an extra *inch* around the edges and the quilt shifts out of line, it can be trimmed to be perfectly square. For a machine-embroidered and worked quilt, trimming the edges is absolutely safe: If you've spent any time with a seam ripper, you know that machine stitching often doesn't need to be knotted to be pretty permanent.

Cutting off the edges of a quilt won't weaken the quilting. All the edges with loose thread will be encased by the binding. Plan your quilt so you can trim.

Using a rotary cutter, a cutting mat, and an acrylic ruler ensures straight lines when I trim my quilts. I lay the quilt on the mat, lined up as closely as possible to the mat's grid. Using the wide flat part of the ruler, I smooth the surface against the table, checking to see that there are no excessively large waves or distortions. If the quilt lies flat, I trim.

Usually there's one side where the details are a little too close to the edge. It's best to start trimming with that one. Lining up the ruler with the grid lines on the mat, I make my first cut, being sure to trim away all excess batting and backing. Using my ruler as a T square, I place it at a 90° angle to the first cut. I make the second cut and then trim the other two sides in the same way.

FIXING WAVY QUILTS

A lot of heavily machine-embroidered quilts lie unevenly in waves. If you've tried the techniques described above and waves are still a problem, there are other answers. You can gather the quilt into a binding or add another backing.

GATHERING INTO THE BINDING

After you've trimmed the quilt, move a large acrylic ruler along the edges of the piece to identify wavy areas. Mark those areas with straight pins. Place a heavy thread, such as cordonnet, gimp, or perle cotton, between the pins, about 1/2" inside the edge. Using all-purpose thread, zigzag over the heavy thread. Take care not to stitch *into* the heavy thread.

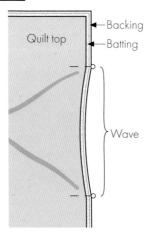

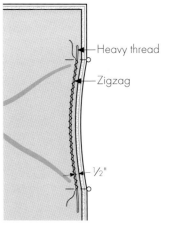

Pull the heavy thread until the wave lies flat, and then twist the thread ends around the pins to anchor them. At this point, you can trim the quilt as described above. Remove the thread and gathering stitches after you have bound the quilt and added a rod pocket (see page 110).

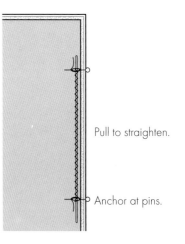

REBACKING

If your quilt is very wavy and you need to gather more than one-quarter of a side's length, you might consider rebacking. I used to do this all the time. Yes, I know, adding another backing is a really desperate measure, but it works! Should you find yourself with a quilt that ruffles and won't lie flat any other way, try rebacking. It's saved several quilts I would otherwise have tossed out.

I tape backing fabric tightly to the table or work surface, right side down. I place a layer of very stiff nonfusible interfacing on top. I put my quilt on the interfacing, right side up, and baste the layers together every 4" with #1 safety pins or with QuilTaks. Using monofilament nylon thread in a straight stitch, I stitch around all the large images in the quilt so the layers are held together. As I quilt, I ease the ruffled parts with my fingers. If one edge is quite ruffled, I run a zigzag stitch over cord (see "Gathering into the Binding" above) to gather it. Then I steam the quilt heavily. Once quilted, my piece should lie remarkably flat, and can easily be trimmed.

This method has saved quilts I thought were irredeemable. It's a last resort, but one worth the trouble.

Adding Rod Pockets

Most quilt shows insist that each quilt have a rod pocket. This is a tube sewn to the top back of the quilt in which a hanging rod can be inserted. If you add the pocket before attaching the binding, you can stitch in place with the binding. Since most quilt shows request a 3"- to 4"-wide tube, I make my strip 8" wide to be on the safe side.

2½" 2½"

Rod pocket

Cut an 8"-wide strip that is 2" shorter than the width of the quilt. Narrowly hem both short ends of the strip with monofilament nylon or neutral-colored thread. Fold the tube in half lengthwise and press it flat with an iron. Center the tube at the top back of the quilt, raw edges matching the raw edges of the quilt. Attach a walking foot to the machine so the layers won't shift as you stitch, and sew the tube to the quilt.

For larger quilts, I sew rod pockets to the top *and* bottom. I insert a heavy rod in the bottom pocket so the quilt will hang evenly.

If you didn't attach the binding at the same time as the rod pocket, bind the edges before anchoring the rod pocket. To anchor the rod pocket, I use monofilament nylon thread in both the top and bobbin of the machine. Select a blind hemstitch and put the blind-hem foot on the machine.

Fold the top of the quilt to the front at the folded edge of the rod pocket. The tube will lie underneath, like the hem of a skirt that you're blind hemstitching. Stitch so that the straight stitches of the blind hemstitch run along the hanging tube, and the little points just nip into the quilt. The quilt is thick enough that the stitches are hidden in the batting.

If you gathered the edges of the quilt to correct waves, now is the time to pull out the gathering thread.

Fold quilt to front.

Back of quilt

Rod pocket

Blind hemstitch

Afterword

Quilts come to life for me in time and space: records and expressions of myself, much like my strand of "memory beads." As for all creations, their purposes and places in the world are past planning. Like the strand of beads, I set the quilts before you with no beginnings or endings. They are each a part of the ongoing process that fills my hands, my heart, and my soul.

Quilt Exhibition

Snake in the Grass, page 9
Publications: *Patchwork Quilt Tsushin* no. 46 (winter 1992): page 44.
American Quilter vol. 8, no. 2 (summer 1992): page 19.

Morning Glories, page 13
Publications: *Patchwork Quilt Tsushin* no. 74, Tokyo (fall 1996): page 121.

Fired Elementals, page 17
Publications: *Quilting International* no. 28 (March 1993): page 34.

In the Clearing, page 21
Publications: *Surface Design Journal* vol. 18, no. 2 (winter 1994): page 25.
Quilting International no. 28 (March 1993): page 32.

Twilight Time, page 22
Awards: Ashville Quilt Show, 1994: Ashville, North Carolina (third place)

Growing Between the Cracks, page 24
Publications: *Patchwork Quilt Tsushin* no. 74, Tokyo (fall 1996): page 121.

Jump at the Sun, page 27
Publications: *Quilter's Gallery* (1996), "Inspired by Nature," Ann Fahl: page 19.

Skimming the Surface, page 28
Publications: *Patchwork Quilt Tsushin* no. 74, Tokyo (fall 1996): page 121.
Quilter's Gallery (1996), "Inspired by Nature," Ann Fahl: page 21.

The Problem with Princes, page 31
Publications: *Quilter's Newsletter Magazine*, issue 291, vol. 28, no. 3 (April 1997): page 35.

Living on the Edge, page 35
Awards: A Quilter's Gathering, 1993: Westford, Massachusetts (craftsmanship)

Quiltfest, 1993: Jacksonville, Florida (second place, machine wall hangings)
Whitewater Textile and Fiber Exhibition, 1994: Whitewater, Wisconsin (certificate of merit for machine embroidery)
Publications: *Threads* no. 5 (July 1994): back cover.

Father of All Fishes, page 45
Publications: *Patchwork Quilt Tsushin* no. 46, Tokyo (winter 1992): page 47.

Breaking the Ice, page 44
Awards: Ashville Quilt Festival, 1993: Ashville, North Carolina (best original design)
Publications: *Quilting International* no. 34 (March 1994): page 48.
Quilting Today no. 41 (April 1994): page 23.
Threads no. 53 (July 1994): back cover.
If Quilts Could Talk (1994 Land's End address book): page G.

Spring Running, page 46
Publications: *Patchwork Quilt Tsushin* no. 74, Tokyo (fall 1996): page 121.
Quilter's Gallery (1996), "Inspired by Nature," Ann Fahl: page 21.

Silent Splendor, page 57
Awards: Quilt Plano, 1991: Plano, Texas (first place, machine appliqué)

Secret Garden, page 52
Awards: Quiltfest, 1994: Louisville, Kentucky (first place, small wall hangings)
Publications: *Fiberarts* vol. 21, no. 2 (September/October 1994): "Profile Ellen Eddy—Quilts from the Deep," page 14.
Art/Quilt Magazine no. 2 (1995): page 22.

Coral Sea, page 51
Publications: *Patchwork Quilt Tsushin* no. 74, Tokyo (fall 1996): page 121.

Resources

THREAD

HERSHEY LEVINSON
1455 West Hubbard Street, Chicago, Illinois 60622
312-226-7100
Rayon and polyester threads, some wrapped metallic threads, embroidery accessories, Pellon products, irons and scissors

MADEIRA USA
30 Bayside Court, Laconia, New Hampshire 03246
800-225-3001
Stabilizers and metallic, rayon, polyester, and cotton threads

SULKY OF AMERICA
3113 Broadpoint Drive, Harbor Heights, Florida 33983
800-874-4115
Rayon, wound metallic, and flat metallic threads; Totally Stable and Solvy stabilizers; and embroidery accessories

YLI CORPORATION
161 West Main Street, Rock Hill, South Carolina 29730
803-985-3100
Perle rayons, Candlelight, Single Ply, Wonder (monofilament nylon), and cotton quilting threads

KREINIK
3106 Timanus Lane, Suite 101, Baltimore, Maryland 21244
800-354-4255
Metallic and silk threads

FABRIC AND DYES

TEST FABRICS
PO Box 420, Middlesex, New Jersey 08846
908-469-6446
Excellent source for ready-to-dye fabrics

DHARMA TRADING COMPANY
PO Box 150916, San Rafael, California 94915
800-542-5227
Excellent dyes, ready-to-dye fabric, and ready-to-dye-and-wear clothing

PRO CHEMICAL AND DYE
PO Box 14, Sommerset, Massachusetts 02726
800-228-9393
Fabric inks, dyes, and dyeing tools

Selected Titles from Fiber Studio Press and That Patchwork Place

FIBER STUDIO PRESS

Complex Cloth: A Comprehensive Guide to Surface Design • Jane Dunnewold
Erika Carter: Personal Imagery in Art Quilts • Erika Carter
Inspiration Odyssey: A Journey of Self-Expression in Quilts • Diana Swim Wessel
The Nature of Design • Joan Colvin
Thread Magic: The Enchanted World of Ellen Anne Eddy • Ellen Anne Eddy
Velda Newman: A Painter's Approach to Quilt Design • Velda Newman
    with Christine Barnes

Appliqué in Bloom • Gabrielle Swain
Bargello Quilts • Marge Edie
Blockbender Quilts • Margaret J. Miller
Color: The Quilter's Guide • Christine Barnes
Colourwash Quilts • Deirdre Amsden
Freedom in Design • Mia Rozmyn
Hand-Dyed Fabric Made Easy • Adriene Buffington
Machine Needlelace and Other Embellishment Techniques • Judy Simmons
Quilted Sea Tapestries • Ginny Eckley
Watercolor Impressions • Pat Magaret & Donna Slusser
Watercolor Quilts • Pat Magaret & Donna Slusser

Many titles are available at your local quilt shop or
where fine books are sold. For more information,
write for a free color catalog to That Patchwork Place, Inc.,
PO Box 118, Bothell, Washington 98041-0118 USA.

U.S. and Canada, call 1-800-426-3126 for the name
and location of the quilt shop nearest you.
Int'l: 1-425-483-3313 Fax: 1-425-486-7596
E-mail: info@patchwork.com
Web: www.patchwork.com